My Fling on the Farm

Patricia Bredin MacCulloch

NIMBUS PUBLISHING LIMITED

Nimbus Publishing Limited
P.O. Box 9301, Station A
Halifax, N.S.
B3K 5N5

Cover Design: Arthur Carter, Halifax
Cover Photograph: by Lorne Rogers, taken at "Ran-Mar" Farm, N.S.
Design: Kathy Kaulbach, Halifax

Canadian Cataloguing in Publication Data

MacCulloch, Patricia

My Fling on the Farm

ISBN 0-921054-18-1

1. MacCulloch, Patricia. 2. Farm life—Nova Scotia—Anecdotes.
I. Title.

S522.C2M33 1989 630'.2'017 C89-098541-3

Printed and Bound in Canada

Nimbus Publishing Limited gratefully acknowledges the support of the Canada Council and the Nova Scotia Cultural Affairs Division.

CONTENTS

DEDICATION

I dedicate this book to my agent from my show-biz days, Joy Jameson, a splendid and vivacious gal with verve, style and vision. (It was she who launched Sean Connery of 007 fame into stellar orbit.) Her notes and occasional letters showed me the amazing power of the pen and the visual images words can reveal, something which years of schooling didn't impart. One could always see Joy as you read her communications. They were so vivid, alive and expressive. Even these many years later, every time I write a note or a letter, she flashes into my mind ... Isn't life extraordinary? I guarantee that no one will be more surprised by this dedication than Joy. I send her my love and thanks. I have to say that there is no link whatsoever between Joy and anything to do with cows or farming. She is an elegant city dweller, and I am sure she would die if confronted by one of my Bovine Beauties.

PREFACE

This book is written firstly as a *crie de coeur* and, more importantly, as a tribute to the farming gals of the world, such as Peggy Rockefeller of New York, who breeds splendid Simmental beef cattle. Like the rest of the "beefaholics," she dotes on her critters and does great things for the improvement of beef in a very elegant way. This is also a tribute to the hard-working, devoted gals, such as Elsie Bond of Nova Scotia, who works from morn to night tending her absolutely superior herd of milkshake suppliers (Jersey cows) with loving dedication. Not least, this book is written as a tribute to those people who can't afford to be farmers but who are smitten with the farming bug and keep a few critters just for the pure love of them. Oddly enough, all of us bovine lovers are seemingly normal, responsible people. But don't be fooled—we are all quite insane because we are smitten with a disease called "Cows."

It just isn't possible to explain why we farmers will sit up all night in the bitter cold of winter helping and encouraging our Mums-2-B through a long labour or slave from dawn to dusk to bring in hay under a sizzling hot summer sun. Why, oh why, I repeatedly ask myself, could I not have been content to focus my boundless love on a single horse, or even two ... why did it have to be sixty hefty four-legged critters whose main occupations were eating and pooping?

Why did I worry myself sick if my critters so much as looked as if they were going to cough? Truly, I just don't know.

But cows are therapy, believe it or not. Tending to their needs soothes the soul. If you think the world is at odds with you, I heartily recommend you acquire a few to take your mind off your troubles. A twenty-four-hour stint of winter calving problems will put things in true perspective.

If we all had to experience at least two years of farming, we would begin to appreciate the things which are so often taken for granted. Hearing a chap recently complaining about having to work past five o'clock made me see red. When I suggested that he should thank his lucky stars he wasn't a farmer working a twenty-four-hour winter day in a barn without central heating, he looked at me with a mixture of puzzlement, disgust and disbelief. I think that most people don't think farmers are for real unless we have straw sticking out from behind our ears.

Before I became a farmer, I too had no idea how hard a life farming is or what dedication it requires. This vocation demands absolute sacrifice. There's none of that "Let's get away for the weekend" stuff or "Where shall we spend the winter this year" nonsense. There can't be when one's shirt-tails are tied to the hay fork and manure scrapper. Only now, still wearing the calluses of hard work on my hands, do I appreciate so many things that "non-farmers" take for granted. Things like clean water running from a tap or not having to climb up on a tractor before dawn to snow-plough a path from the house to the barn. Will I ever get used to finding a carton of milk in the refrigerator which I didn't personally take from a cow on a bitterly cold morning after first having to gently massage her udder to bring warmth back to it, my own fingers just about as cold as her udder. Can I forget what life is like in mid-winter (which seems to be most of the year in Nova Scotia) to dig my way through high drifts of snow (the tractor having succumbed to the cold) only to find a deep frozen water supply and sixty thirsty hefty gals needing to drink. Oh God, I hate Canadian winters!

How far away seemed my days of luxury, when even to think the words "oh shit" would have made me recoil from such profanities in horror. Well, all I can tell you is that being in the middle of a manure pile, perched on a stalled tractor, in a driving gale, will cure you of any such delicacies of mind. So will absent-mindedly touching the electric fence after you have just spent the last two hours fixing it! The zap from that little bout of forgetfulness will curl the hair on even the baldest of heads.

My original title for this book was *Oh Shit*—two words which catch the essence of what looking after cows is all about. Then I moved on to the title *The Spelling's Atrocious* after my editor's first reaction to the manuscript. My heart went out to her. Spelling is all very well, but I have gone way past that ... why, I am up to the eyebrows in degrees. What does spelling matter when you have every farming degree in the book? Along with Don Herron of television fame, I have my B.S. (Bull Shit), M.S. (More of the Same) and Ph.D. (Piled Higher and Deeper) from the "Barn of Achievement" and the "Fields of Endeavour." Not only that, I have earned a D.D. (Dumb and Dedicated) with the shovel, and there are not that many of us about, I can tell you.

But pray tell me, now that my farming days are over, why do I miss my Gals ... my two thousand pounders of aggravation, pooping and eating? Truly, Cows is a disease for which there is no cure, and my heart will always bleed a little for their departing.

Life is indeed one long journey of discovery. I discovered, to my surprise, that all of the cartoons showing farmers leaning over their fences, watching their cows, were based upon reality. Taking the time to observe the herd is vitally important in farming, because a critter's behaviour tells a great deal about its well-being. Only by observing them can you detect anything amiss. Besides, seeing the young ones running about in the pasture under the summer sun, with their little tails lifted high in the air or flicking from side to side as they suckle their mothers, brings joy to the heart. And, oh, it feels so good to lean comfortably against a fence, giving the blisters and calluses a rest while enjoying the rewards of one's labours.

Fences are important to us farmers ... and while we're on the subject, read me kindly, I beg you, from your side of the fence.

Patricia MacCulloch
North West Cove, N.S.

ABOUT ME

I loathe discussing me; however, my trusted editor asked for a self-portrait, so here it is. I was born (and brought up) in England, on St. Valentine's day, and I just adore my birthday. No matter how long in the tooth I become, I will always be a birthday girl. It is such fun getting Valentine and birthday cards at the same time, and my friends usually give me a party with lots of champagne, balloons and crazy gifts.

Early in life, by order of Mama, I took piano lessons. For seven long years I suffered them. To my unfortunate piano teacher (by the name of Mrs. Moor) it probably seemed like seven thousand years, and eventually she just couldn't take any more and suggested that she play and I sing. This excellent solution to both our problems worked out famously. Soon her usual welcoming scowl was replaced with a sunny smile, and the formerly long hours of misery became enjoyable fleeting moments of mutual pleasure. My singing days had begun.

I sang in the church choir and the amateur dramatic society and then won a Golden Voice competition, the prize for which was a broadcast. This led to broadcasts on an ongoing basis. Then I met a wonderful Australian opera singer, Alice Gange, who introduced me to Alexander Faris, a conductor who was later to write the music of the popular TV series "Upstairs, Downstairs." I sang for him. A couple of weeks later I received a telegram informing me that one of the cast of the successful musical he was conducting, "Wedding in Paris," was leaving and replacement auditions were to be held. I auditioned, along with five hundred other hopefuls, got the job, and some three weeks later the impresarios put me under contract and sent me to the Central School of Drama. We had lessons in the Royal Albert Hall in London. I was always late and could never remember in which room we were scheduled to be. The Royal Albert Hall is a huge round building some seven or eight stories high, and all of the rooms look alike. So I did an almost daily gallop, round and round and up and up, looking for my class. I became so fit I could have won the Derby. That was during the day; at night I did the show. On the tour I was given the juvenile lead. It was so exciting performing with the legendary Anton Walbrook and Evelyn Laye. Then I got an agent, Joy (to whom this book is dedicated), who made a two-and-sixpenny bet with a casting agent that if he would agree to meet me, he would cast me. Bless her, she won her bet!

To my amazement and delight I was cast opposite Roger Moore, playing the lead in an episode of his popular television series "Lancelot." The episode was entitled "The Gentle Jester," and I was that gentle jester. In real life Roger Moore, with quite the bluest sparkling eyes I have ever seen, is even more handsome and charming than he is in the movies. He was so kind and helpful to me because I had never been on a film set before. He was my first "Lancelot" of show-biz days. I can't recall the plot, but I do remember the costume; it had countless bells on it. I spent a week in that costume ding-donging from hither to thither and could even hear those bells in my sleep. Who would ever have thought that I would have something in common with the old actor Charles Laughton ... The Bells ... The Bells ... Oh, the Bells!

After that I played leading roles in several films and

appeared on countless television shows. Looking back, I think it's quite extraordinary how I seem to have become the subject of bets. I recall that BBC-TV producer Francis Essex came to see a stage musical that I was appearing in at the Savoy Theatre in London called "Free As Air." At that time the BBC was preparing to do the very first live link-up of television across Europe. It was as exciting as going to the moon was in later years. It seems that the established singing stars of the day had all refused to sing a particular song which had been selected, and Francis, after seeing "Free As Air," offered me my first television appearance, conditional upon my agreeing to sing the song that no-one else would sing. I was delighted to sing the sweet simple ballad called "All."

There was much hurrah about the final show, which was to be "judged" by popular response. All of the musically important people in the business were there, and of course it was live. Francis took a bet of ten pounds that I would win the competition, and I am delighted to report that he also won his bet, because I did win, by a landslide popular round-Britain vote, and went romping off to Germany to represent England in the first-ever Eurovision Festival of Song, accompanied by a vast British contingent flying the flag in true British style. The show was televised from Frankfurt, but I can't spell the name of the place where it was held. I do recall its translation into English, which was "Dogs Heaven." The building had a great number of large golden pillars, and seemingly, when dogs die, they look forward to being rewarded by great numbers of golden trees in the great hereafter ... which makes me think that it may be only male dogs who go to heaven. The orchestra was certainly heavenly; there were about 160 players, and the strings just sang—they were too wonderful for words. After I had rehearsed, I was terribly embarrassed when the whole orchestra stood and applauded me ... something which is a tremendous honour among musicians. I was so young and inexperienced, I just didn't know what to do. Needless to say the British contingent was highly delighted. It was a wonderful experience.

During my twenty-year career, I did many stage, film, TV and cabaret shows. In fact, my very first cabaret date was on New Year's Eve at London's Claridges Hotel, nicknamed "The Hotel of Kings," and you can't get more prestigious than that. I've done Royal Command performances at Theatre Royal Windsor (which was quite near my home in Gerrards Cross in Buckinghamshire) and at Buckingham Palace, and eventually I took over the role of Queen Guenevere from Julie Andrews in the Broadway, New York, musical production of "Camelot," where my second show-biz Lancelot was Robert Goulet, whose singing was glorious.

In show business you either make big money or peanuts, and I am happy to report that I did the former. Money was never my god; I earned it, I spent it and had a wonderful life singing in countries all over the world. I confess to being wild, impulsive and headstrong, along with being carefree and happy. I breezed about in a happy haze, singing for my supper and enjoying life to the fullest.

When I was young, I played very serious tennis for hours on end and never tired. I do have boundless energy, which comes in handy for long rehearsals. I recall at one stage in my life I was up at dawn, filming all day, playing in a London musical in the evening and then doing two cabarets at the Savoy Hotel at night.

I have never smoked, except once, aged eleven, in a graveyard with other naughty youngsters, and that cured me for life. For the first twenty-six years of my life I didn't drink, having been a red-hot Methodist and Sunday school-teacher. My farming adventures later proved to me that a good stiff drink can soothe the soul, and I have found that champagne is one of the better staffs of life.

My life has always been filled with music; it is my first love. My passions are Bellini, Verdi, Puccini and Mozart, along with Streisand and Shirley Bassey. Although piano lessons were a chore, I have never been able to exist without a piano. I bought my first "own" piano (a nine-foot grand) at an auction sale and recall being over the moon with delight when the bidding stopped at ten pounds. It was the joy of my life and cost more than its purchase price to get it home.

It was indeed a little older than any piano I had ever played, and a few of the notes didn't work, but it was my very own, and I was thrilled with it. Not long after purchasing it, I went away to do a summer season, and when I returned in the autumn, I could hardly believe my eyes: my adored treasure had collapsed! There it was—a heap of junk. Only then did I learn of the existence in this world of wood-worms. The little blighters had had a fiesta while I was away, actually eating the huge main supporting beam, which had to have come from one of the mightier oaks of England. There was almost nothing left of it except a pile of dust. Well, that was the *morte de piano*, so I got a little man to take the remains away. He had said it would cost a pound, but when he saw my sad young face, he gave me a pound instead—for my helping him load it into his truck.

The turning point in my life came in 1970. I was on the first world cruise of the *QE II*. It was so exciting, a very prestigious affair with Britain showing the rest of the world that she still ruled the waves. Anyone who considered themselves to be anyone was on board. There was a splendid mixture of fascinating people, and we were afforded all of the pomp and circumstance that Mother England could dream up. To top it all off, I met the world's most perfect man, and you can't ask for better than that!

We were playing a deck game, and I was partnered with a handsome, distinguished stranger who looked remarkably like Clark Gable. I learned that he was from Nova Scotia, which didn't mean a lot to me—I vaguely remembered seeing it on a map somewhere. Certainly I did not dream that this chance meeting on board the world's newest and

The little cottage I first came to at Monte Vista.

most glamorous ocean liner would change my life completely and that I would eventually be raising beef cattle on a Nova Scotia farm.

Suffice to say that the handsome stranger and I were eventually married at our lovely Monte Vista Estate—two thousand acres set on the shore of Grand Lake in Nova Scotia—and we were blissfully happy. We also had our own Caribbean island, Young Island, off St. Vincent in the West Indies. Life was a romantic whirl of entertaining, travelling, tennis, golf, music, dancing, love and laughter. If I had a problem, it was only as serious as choosing what to wear for any new and wonderful occasion. Monte Vista was our earthly paradise. It had been an ancient Indian mystical place, and I could well imagine why. It seemed to enclose one with invisible arms of love so that you would never want to leave. And so it was with us.

When we first went to Monte Vista, it was a collection of small farms owned by a chap named Horn, the man who first discovered Noranda Mines. He spent most of his life prospecting and then at the age of sixty came to Monte Vista. We

The elegant home we created on the shores of Long Lake.

"played" house there and then improved and expanded the main house until it became a splendid and elegant home. The land was so beautiful, with wooded rolling hills, a delightful river and half a mile of waterfalls—a second Eden. We planted gardens around the house and cultivated about fifty acres into a golf course with a putting green and a tennis court. There were many bays along the six miles of lake frontage; the one in front of the main house was shallow and sandy-shored, delightful for youngsters to paddle in. Wildlife abounded. I was amazed to discover how quickly a snapping turtle could run across a field and fascinated by the skill of beavers as they built their homes in the lake, from huge trees they cut down with only their teeth.

We were so busy building our own nest we didn't begin thinking of a honeymoon until some sixteen months after we were married. We decided that because we had met on a cruise, we would go on one for our honeymoon. We chose the South Pacific. It was everything we could have dreamed of … and then my darling suddenly died, and part of my soul died with him.

Perhaps it is a bad thing to have everything in life, the perfect love, the perfect lifestyle, I don't know. I do know that when I lost my love, I had nothing that gave me reason to live. I merely existed, in a blur of grief. I did not want to cope with life without him, and yet I continued to go on living. Day followed day, and somehow cope I did.

Then for reasons neither I nor anyone else could understand, I buried myself in cows. Cows, of all things! Not just the odd horse or two, but huge cows and countless numbers of them …

THE BEGINNING

It was late in 1979, after the death of my husband, and the beginning of vast legal problems involving his estate, that my farming life began. The stark horror of losing my husband, who was everything in the world to me, was completely devastating! It was as if one half of me had been chopped off, the half that was warm, vital, fun, exciting and necessary, leaving behind only a cold shell. The reality of being alone, of not having his loving arms around me, of not being protected and cared for was unbearable. I had never experienced this type of reality, because I had not led a normal life. I had never paid a household bill. I had no idea what things cost. I was alone in a foreign land with no idea of how to cope. And yet, completely unprepared for this kind of life, I went into farming. It was an escape from my loneliness and misery.

This is how it happened. Shortly after my adored husband's death the couple who managed the estate announced that they were expecting their first baby. Timmy, the husband, very reasonably asked for a raise in his salary. The executors of the estate, being full of goodwill and generosity, wouldn't give him one. (I felt very badly about this because I was one of the four executors, but my pleas on his behalf fell on deaf ears.) When Timmy came to me to complain, I tried to help as best I could. I pointed out that we had lots of land and good big barns, and I suggested he get some "hay burners," young calves which he could feed and sell to make extra money. He was delighted with the idea.

I was surprised when he arrived home one day in November with three day-old calves. I had assumed he would get animals which were old enough to eat hay. Even I knew that babies, no matter whose, needed mothers' milk to help immunize them from disease. I pointed out to him that our Jersey cow, the household milk and cream supply, was "dry" and that there was thus no milk for the little creatures. He cheerfully informed me that he had bought a large bag of dried milk powder to feed them with. As he was obviously thrilled with his purchases, I congratulated him and thought no further about the matter.

About two weeks later my dear friends Andrea and Sherman Hines, who had had a death in the family, asked if I would sing at the funeral. How could I refuse. This was a depressing task, coming so soon after my husband's death, but it was something I couldn't get out of, so I obliged. I certainly didn't need the shock of being wakened the following morning at 6:15 by a great crash.

I shot out of bed and went to investigate the cause and discovered that the kitchen ceiling had fallen down because of a water-pipe freeze-up. It had been a false ceiling, built much lower than the original higher one, and whoever had built it had left the clutter and junk of the ages up there.

Down it had all come with an avalanche of icy water. I took one look and surprised myself by deciding that I couldn't cope and went back to bed. It is extraordinary how the mind switches itself off when it can't take any more stress. At 8:00 Timmy came over, looking very down at the mouth. I didn't expect him to be thrilled with the mess of the burst water pipe, but it seemed to me that something else was the cause of his despondency. My suspicions were well founded. Hardly seeming to notice the devastation around us, he gazed at me with a look that said more than words. When he finally spoke, it was to tell me that his calves were sick. "Oh dear," I sighed, "but maybe it was something to be expected after all, they were so young. What is wrong with them?" I was told that the barn was too cold for them. I hadn't the faintest idea what conditions young calves needed but asked if I could be of any help. It turned out that I could, by allowing them into the only place warm enough for them: my basement. Heavens, that was the least I could do. I immediately offered the basement as their new home, and in the rush to install them there, we both forgot instantly about the wreckage in the kitchen, even though water was running down the walls and we were wading about in it.

Timmy went off to the barn for the calves and for straw to make up their beds. When I saw the animals, I was shocked. They were so terribly ill. One little black-and-white one was bleeding from the rear end, another one was making awful noises gasping for breath, and the third was twitching. "Oh God," I thought, "they're dying." Then, trying not to look as bad as I felt, I volunteered to rush them to a vet. It certainly didn't look as though we had time to wait around for a vet to come to us. Our estate was located in a remote area some thirty-five miles from the nearest town. It is truly amazing how fast one's brain whirls in an emergency. "Put some straw in my car," I said. "You'll have to stay here and sort out this mess with the plumber. I'm no good at plumbing, but I can drive."

In a flash, my Mercedes sports car was filled with straw and calves. The black-and-white one, still squirting blood from its rear end, was put in the back seat with the twitching one, and the dark-red-and-white one, wheezing horribly, was put on the passenger seat next to me. Those awful wheezing, gasping noises made me shiver with horror. It sounded like its lungs were about to burst.

I don't know why, but before I got into the car, I had

dashed into the house and grabbed some newspaper to stuff between the door and around the back of my neck. That turned out to be a stroke of genius.

I set off at the speed of sound with everything squirting in every direction. God, what a mess and what a smell! I couldn't open the window at my side, because the newspaper I had stuffed into the space between the car and the window would fly out, and I didn't dare open the one on the passenger side in case it gave a draft to the calves. So with every possibility of my lungs not lasting the trip, we disappeared into the blue yonder in the direction of Halifax.

The first seven or so miles were dirt road; calves bounced in every direction as we hit the potholes. "Tough bananas, duckies," I thought to myself. What were a few bumps and bruises in a matter of life and death? Things got a bit better when we hit the highway, but at this point it dawned upon me that I didn't know where on earth to find a vet. Fortunately there was a telephone in the car, and surrounded by calves, with the gas pedal pressed to the floor, I dialed Information. It took me quite some time to explain to the operator that no, I was not in a telephone booth, that I was travelling at high speed along a highway in a car full of sick calves and that I was desperately trying to find my way to a vet to get them treated. I think at first she thought it was some weird joke, but the urgency in my voice finally convinced her to help me. She directed me street by street to the vet's surgery. By now there was a terrible mess in the car. When cows or calves are upset, they poop at a ninety-degree angle. I thanked Fate for the newspaper shielding my head, neck and shoulders. I prefer Chanel to Sh— anytime.

It is interesting how one's attitude changes according to circumstances. Normally I would have been appalled at the thought of all that mess in my splendid 450 SLC Mercedes sports car; now, who gave a damn? The calves' lives were at stake. All that mattered was getting them to a vet before they died.

We seemed to be in luck; the vet's place was not far from the highway exit. We screamed to a halt, I leapt out of the car and shot inside the door of the surgery. I almost dragged the poor young vet out by the ears. To my intense irritation, he didn't seem at all frantic or het up, as I most certainly was. He was quite calm and unexcited, not at all impressed with the life-and-death situation. I was almost doing a war dance! He looked at the calves nonchalantly and said, "They don't really have a chance. They are too far gone." "What?!" I exclaimed. Was the fellow a lunatic? They were still breathing, admittedly not with ease, indeed loudly and spasmodically, but breathing nevertheless. "You can't just let them die! There must be something you can do!" I insisted. Still calm, and with not very great enthusiasm, he went back into the building. I followed him, my hands itching to choke him. I couldn't trust myself to speak. He disappeared into his surgery, and I could do nothing but wait outside, willing myself not to bash the door in. Pacing outside the closed doors, I got an inkling of what an expectant father goes through. He trudged back out with various things. How anyone could be so calm under such desperate circumstances was beyond me. Of course it didn't occur to me that he saw such dramas daily. I was new at this game and certainly not in the calm-and-detached league.

I trailed him back to the car. Suddenly I realized he wasn't even going to help me take them out of the car into the surgery. "There's no point in taking them out," he said. "Wot?" My jaw hung, my mind black with rage. Did this man not realize that his own life was in danger—and from me? Fortunately, before it got to manslaughter, he started to attend to them. He took their temperatures and gave them a number of injections as I hovered like a demented mother hen, asking questions about everything he did to them. I couldn't complain about the very gentle way in which he handled the calves, and my blinding rage began to abate. When he had finished treating them, I followed him back into his office, where my voice returned, and I demanded more information. What was I to do with them, what medication was he going to give me, and how would I give it to them? As I was bombarding him with questions, he was putting together a collection of medications and writing the instructions on the bottles and packages. These he packed, along with needles and syringes, into a brown paperbag and handed it to me. Then, as I stood with my mouth open like a total twit, he wished me well, calmly turned on his heel and went to attend to another unfortunate.

Heavens, it was shades of being dumped at school by Nanny and left to get on with it! Sputtering like a damp firecracker, I returned to the car, my mind reeling. I still couldn't understand why he hadn't been in total trauma, as I was—it was unreal—how could he not at least sob or howl or jump up and down?... Of course it didn't occur to me that he was in fact behaving like a good efficient vet and that I was a complete pain in the rear end.

In a sort of trance, I drove off with the three calves. I couldn't believe that we had actually managed to get to a vet and get them treated and that we were now on our way back home. This time I didn't drive at the speed of sound but slowly and with great care.

As I drove on with my precious cargo, my fury abated, and I turned my attention to the sick trio. I noticed a change—a threatening lull in the noises they were making. The terrible harsh, rasping gasps of the calf lying on the passenger seat beside me had quietened, and there was no sound from the two in the back. Immediate panic! My heart started to pound furiously—I was sure they were dying. The pathetic little creature lying on the seat next to me now just lay limply; it had stopped gasping. "Oh God, oh God, let them live," I prayed, with tears falling down my cheeks. "What more could I do," I wondered as I turned on to the dirt road to the farm.

As I drove up to the main house, I saw Timmy waiting

there with a strained, bleak expression on his face. Obviously he feared the worst. Goodness only knows what my face looked like. Neither of us spoke. As I got out, he reached into the car and very gently picked up the calf from the front passenger seat. I followed them down to the basement, where he had their beds of straw ready for them. Then I followed him back out to the car, and he reached into the back to pick up another calf. I helped hold the front seat out of the way, and having something to do brought my voice back. I started to tell him what had happened. He carried the last of them down into the basement and laid it tenderly down on to the dry sweet-smelling straw. There the three of them lay, quiet and still. My heart almost burst in my chest, fearing that they might be dead. I reached out and touched one—it was still breathing! "It's still alive," I said as the tears flowed freely. "I thought they were dead." I started to sob, and Timmy explained that it was the medication taking effect, and then we all lapsed again into silence.

We both sat down on the straw beside the sleeping calves, and then Cutler, my huge Lassie-type dog, came bounding down the basement stairs to join the party. Wooffee!!! His great joyous bark jolted us. It broke the terrible silent sadness. He was absolutely delighted with the newcomers. He wagged his tail with delight as he sniffed them, quite clearly convinced that they were there especially for him. Indeed one would have thought that he had given birth to them himself. Gratefully I reached out to him, putting my arms around his wonderfully thick, furry neck. I hugged him tightly. There was no fear of him dying, thank the Lord. Timmy also had tears running unashamedly on his face. I buried mine in Cutler's long fur. I explained to him that he had a very special job; that from now on, he had three lovely babies to love and look after; that he was to guard them and keep them safe. Oh, how that tail wagged! It was a wonder it didn't succeed in wagging itself off, so delighted a tail it was.

Meanwhile, Timmy and I consoled ourselves by stroking

the calves. I felt so desperately sad for him; he obviously loved them very much. And as for me, I just couldn't countenance more death in my life. It was at that moment that I realized I was totally alone. I was alone, and I was the one who had to make decisions now. It was a terrible and desperately lonely realization.

"Let's have a coffee," I suggested, standing up and heading for the stairs to the kitchen. Timmy followed me up, leaving Cutler to guard the calves. Only vaguely did I notice that the water which had been running down the walls when I had left had now stopped. There was still mess everywhere, and we sloshed about in water, making coffee. The mess all around us was no longer important—keeping those calves alive was all that mattered.

Over coffee, we discussed the problem. Timmy was obviously extremely upset—the calves meant a lot to him. How was I to deal with the situation? I took a deep breath and asked, "How much did you pay for them?" He answered that it was his problem and that he didn't want to burden me with it. Now, I was only too aware that with the coming of their first baby, he and his pretty wife couldn't afford to lose money, especially as he hadn't received his increase in salary. "Look," I said, making my first lone decision, "I want to know how much they've cost you because I insist on buying them."

He stubbornly resisted telling me how much they cost; however, ignoring his objections, I started to write out a cheque and at last, having got the amount out of him, filled it in and insisted that he accept it. We shook hands on the deal. Secretly I was terrified that he wouldn't accept the cheque before the calves died, which I was still sure might happen at any second. After we had struck the deal, we drank our coffee and then went back down into the basement. To my surprise, the calves were still breathing.

The next morning I went down into the basement full of trepidation and was astonished to discover that they were

Learning to drink from a bucket. As the calf sucked my fingers, I lowered its head into the milk.

still alive. It was a miracle! By evening they were beginning
to look a little better. As the days went by, they progressed
beyond our wildest hopes.

Everyone who visited our estate thereafter was taken
(willing or otherwise) down into the basement to see my
new family. There would be dear Cutler, guarding his
buddies with such love and pride. What a wonderful animal
he was, so huge and yet so gentle and loving. His long nose
gave him such an elegant disdainful look, but his appearance completely belied his nature. The calves, for their part,
tolerated him—barely—but, heavens, they grew like mush-
rooms, almost before our very eyes.

Need I say that a greater part of my day from then on was
spent down in the basement. All the calves were brushed
daily until their coats gleamed. It came as a surprise to me
when a friend commented on their size and suggested that
they would soon be too big to get up the stairs and out. That
hadn't occurred to me! It was so pleasant having them down
there—it reminded me of Switzerland, of a place I used to
stay: a small family hotel in a little village where they kept
cows under the house.

How sad the day when we carried them (or rather Timmy
did, with me doing some lifting from behind) up the
basement stairs and back to the barn. We only just got them
out in time, I can tell you. T.L.C. and lots of powdered milk
had done its work. The calves were now glowing with good
health, in spite of being a bit like pin-cushions with the
number of injections they had had. If they had weighed one
ounce more, we would never have got them out.

What a strange void they left. I really missed not having
them in the basement. There was no more of that joyful
rushing down the stairs—even before that morning
"cuppa"—to say "Good morning" to the calves, followed by
ever-faithful Cutler the dog, who had taken it upon himself
to do the daily inspection of sniffing them as his tail wagged
happily. The die was cast, and though at the time I didn't
realize it, my life as a farmer had begun.

THE AUCTION

Being the mother of two dear young calves, I made the barn
my second home. (I couldn't bare the "Oh, how I wish they
were still mine" look on Timmy's face when he was tending
the calves ... so I had given him one of them back.) There
were now two surrogate mums in the barn, Timmy and me!
We developed a great camaraderie. There was the daily
inspection of each other's kin, the "whose best." Need I tell
you that mine were far superior? Timmy, I am sure, was of
the reverse opinion—such is the rivalry of new motherhood. Shortly afterwards he asked if I was interested in
buying any more cows. More cows? Why not? I agreed to go
along with him to the local cattle market. It was held weekly,
on Thursdays. We took the truck, and Timmy attached to
the back of it a double horse trailer borrowed from his
sister.

I didn't quite know cattle-auction protocol, so I wore
what I thought was suitable clothing. This included a cute
velvet baker's-boy cap. I looked quite smart, maybe not
exactly the typical cow-farmer look, but it gave me the right
"down-on-the-farm" feeling. But there was no way I was
going to take off my eleven-carat diamond ring. Any cow of
mine, I decided, would have to put up with such things. So,
done up like a farming-dog's dinner, I joined Timmy, who
was waiting outside in the truck; I climbed aboard and away

we went. The auction place was about an hour away, on the outskirts of the next small town. By now it was mid-December, which in Nova Scotia is a pretty miserable time of the year. True to form, this was a rotten day, blowing snowy sleet, overhung skies, windy ... but none of this could dampen the high spirits of my very first cattle auction. I loved auctions, and I hoped that cows didn't come equipped with woodworm, as I knew from past experience that pianos did. We reached the outskirts of the town and found our way to the auction grounds. We parked amongst the rows of huge cattle trucks, ordinary trucks and cars, then trudged our way through the slush to the entrance.

The place was in three parts. The auction room itself was ringed by a series of concrete steps upon which one sat as in an amphitheatre. At the bottom of the steps was the auction ring, a framework of strong metal bars. At the back of the ring were two gates, an "in" gate and an "out" gate, through which the animals were herded either singly or in groups for the audience to view during the bidding.

Standing in the ring was a chap who carried a stick with which he would prod the poor animals to make them move about the ring, so that prospective purchasers could get a better look at them. Seeing that bloke prodding the already very upset animals made my blood boil! I could see no reason to keep jabbing any creature that way, and it was all I could do to stop myself from going down and boxing his ears. I had to make do with yelling uncontrollably, "Hoi! Stop hitting that cow! How would you like it if you were bashed with a stick?" My remarks attracted very curious stares from the assembled throng, and feeling a bit of a twit, I went into another section, where the cattle were waiting their turn to go into the auction ring. This was a series of strong metal enclosures, up whose bars it was possible to climb to get a better look at the prospective purchases. The third section was the "assorted" section. This contained pens of pretty well everything—goats, sheep, darling piglets, ducks, chickens, hamsters, cats—you name it, it was there.

There was also a primitive canteen serving hamburgers, french fries, tea and coffee. We got our supply and climbed up the concrete steps to choose a place with a good view. The hamburgers tasted jolly good! Our return drew great curiosity from the "usuals," the farmers and dealers who were assembled. I suppose they wondered what extraordinary behaviour I would come up with next. Possibly they weren't used to a gal in an elegant hat and a diamond ring shouting at the chap with the stick because of the way he was bashing the critters. It was a toss-up as to who got the most attention, me or the next animals into the ring.

I soon forgot about the curious stares as the auction commenced. The auctioneer entered his booth at the side of the ring accompanied by two other people, one a lady who wrote busily from the time she sat down, the other a man who scanned the crowd for bidders. It was incredibly difficult to hear what the auctioneer was saying. The public-address system was distorted and loud, and for reasons best known to himself, the auctioneer was yelling in a sort of continuous wailing jabber. Trying to hear what was going on was pretty frustrating for a first-timer. Although it was only about ten in the morning, some of the farmers were in a merry mood, smelling as if they had had an early start at the "wine gums." As it was their one day off in the week, who could blame them for having a party?

As the auction progressed, I noticed two men bidding drunkenly against each other. The auctioneer, upon realizing that they didn't even know what time of day it was, let alone what they were bidding on, was kind enough to stop everything and start again.

Then Fate struck. Four huge gleaming black Aberdeen Angus cows were ushered into the auction ring. It was love at first sight. I realized I just had to have them, so I started to bid. Oh heavens, it was so exciting! Timmy was trying to tell me something, but I wasn't listening ... I was bidding in a state of wild roller-coaster excitement. I was so excited and so determined not to be out-bid that my arms were doing an imitation of Don Quixote's windmills. What Timmy was trying to tell me was that I was bidding against myself. A truly prophetic start to my farming spree.

Anyway, I ended up with those cows. They were mine—four Aberdeen Angus gals—mine, all mine. And the fever had only just started. Timmy explained to me that they were so large because they were pregnant. Pregnant? Not only was I now a mother, but I was about to be a grandmother—my joy knew no bounds.

Timmy was bidding on other young calves, which he fancied, so I went out to the waiting pens to inspect my critters and see that they were gently treated. I warned the cattle handlers what I would do to them if they came anywhere near my four cows with that stick. They obviously thought I was crazy. After giving them their instructions, I went back into the auction room and bought more and more young cows. Oh, it was all so exciting. Soon Timmy pointed out that we just couldn't get any more critters into the transport, and so, reluctantly, I left the ring and went to pay for my purchases.

It is true that time flies when you're having fun, so by now it was quite late in the day. One helluva drama ensued as we loaded up our purchases. First of all we had to find them. As they came out of the auction ring after being sold, they were herded into waiting pens. They had to wait, and you had to wait, until your payment was taken in exchange for a proof-of-purchase chit. This then had to be handed to the chap in charge, who took the chit and helped "fish" your critter out of the milling throng of other critters.

Our problem was that we had so many. I had lost count, as I hadn't taken much interest in what Timmy had bought. We had to have a discussion to sort things out. (All of the other buyers were doing the same thing, but they appeared to have the benefit of past experience.) Timmy found a spot where we could "store" our purchases until it was loading time, and then we went around locating their pens and herding them along the alleyways to the holding pen we had reserved. After we checked our list carefully so that we didn't leave any behind, Timmy disappeared to bring the truck to the loading bay. It was now dark and terribly stormy. My feet were cold even though I had boots on, and I stamped around to try and warm them up. At last Timmy came with the truck and horse-box. Oh boy, they looked pretty small for all of our purchases. We enlisted a couple of willing helpers and set about getting the four pregnant Aberdeen Angus critters into the horse-box for two ... some job, I can tell you. I was terrified that the unborn babies would be crushed. It is one thing getting a very upset animal into a horse-box, but it is quite another keeping it there until you get its three buddies in with it. We had to rush around to find something—anything—to put up alongside the ramp they had to walk up to get into the vehicle so that they didn't fall off the side, or jump off, which they were stupid enough to try to do. At last we got them in, but the horse-box looked as if it would burst at the seams. We borrowed a very long, strong rope, and Timmy wound it around and around the horse-box. It looked like a monster Christmas parcel, one that steamed as it breathed in the bitterly cold night air. Then we turned our attention to the youngsters, who would have to be got into the back of the truck. How we got them in I will never know. They were all crammed in like sardines in a tin. However, there they all were ... boxed in and ready for the road.

It was after seven in the evening by the time we were organized. After thanking our helpers, we climbed into the truck, and the engine was started. I was so excited I couldn't wait to get home. Off we went into the stormy night.

We drove out of the auction yard, and the sleet had turned into snow flurries. As Timmy hadn't turned on the

windscreen wipers, I suggested that maybe he should.
There was an embarrassed silence before I was told that they
didn't work. "Wot?" I asked. "They don't work?" I couldn't
believe it. We were loaded fit to burst, and we couldn't even
see out of the windows on a stormy night with the sleet and
snow coming down more heavily with each passing minute.
How on earth would we get home? A further enquiry
confirmed that we also had no headlights. It was crazy. I
turned around to check on the critters, crammed into the
back of the truck. I prayed that the air in the truck would last
till, or rather if, we got home. It was obviously not a time to
start complaining about truck maintenance; there was
nothing to do but to cross my cold fingers and continue on
into the storm and the night. It was like driving in Braille.

Poor Timmy drove with his head sticking out of the side
window. It took us over two hours to get back home, two
long dreary hours. How we didn't end up in jail I don't
know. But we finally pulled up outside the barn. Oh, the
rejoicing when we unloaded our critters! It was so tremendously exciting—Christmas had come early. We unpacked
the big cows first. They had to be treated very carefully, like
the pregnant ladies they were. The seven others followed,
bursting out of the truck like corks out of champagne
bottles. Eventually they were all safely unloaded and bedded down in their stalls with deep, dry straw to lie on and
plenty of feed to eat. They were so delighted to be in a nice
cosy barn and to be fed and watered. I brushed each one of
mine and told them that I was their new mother and that,
of course, I loved them. It was a wonderful feeling to know
that they were mine and that they were home safe and
sound. I stood listening to the sounds of contented chewing. I was now a real farmer. I had a herd all my own and
babies to come very soon. Could a girl of quality want more
in life?

We all slept warm and contented that night. I was no
longer alone; I had a wonderful new family. Admittedly they

had four legs instead of the usual two, but that was the fun of it, and they were mine, mine, mine. I fell asleep humming (to the tune of "A Life on the Ocean Wave"), "A farmer's life for me, a farmer's life for me!"

BRANCHING OUT

After a year or so, and many local auctions later, I discovered that I had a splendid "eye" for beef. That meant that I could recognize which young animals would become well-formed mature beasts. My "cheapos" grew up to be wonderful, sturdy beef animals of every kind and colour.

One evening I discovered an old beef magazine which had on the front of it the picture of an absolutely splendid cow. A really majestic beast. It was a huge golden-and-white animal. The breed was called Simmental. Suddenly I knew this was the breed I wanted to specialize in. I had pretty well one or two of every breed, as well as a few mongrels, but no particular breed had caught my enthusiasm ... until I spotted the animal on the front of this magazine.

There is no telling why a person prefers one breed of cow to another, just as there is no way of telling why some dog owners prefer poodles and others labradors. I think it's called a "fancy." I liked the fact that the Simmentals were absolutely huge with strong straight backs and true strong legs. There can be nothing spindly about good beef animals; they must be strong and full looking. I don't personally care for the look of the big black-and-white milk cows. They remind me of coat hangers.

I like my critters to look well fed. I like Aberdeen Angus cows, but their legs are comparatively short. I think Simmental cows are more uniform to the eye. Anyway, all breeders have their own reasons for liking a particular type. I discovered that I was a Simmental gal, simple as that. In agricultural lingo, it is one of the "exotic" breeds, and it originated in Germany and Switzerland, where they are used for both beef and milk production.

The fact that the magazine was about eight years out of date didn't matter—that gal on the front was simply splendid, a real bovine beauty queen. I telephoned one of the breeders, in Alberta, and enquired if he still had any of the kind of cows advertised in the particular magazine. His name was Harvey Trimble. He was very pleasant to talk to. Yes, he did have some to sell. "How many have you got to choose from?" I asked. "About eight hundred or so," Harvey answered. My goodness, that was enough for a gal who recognizes quality to choose from, make no mistake. A date was set for me to visit his "spread" near Calgary.

A couple of days later I was off and away. It was time to upgrade my herd. I got quite a surprise when I got to my destination, a place called Okotoks, Alberta. What a spread it was! Why, the office alone was quite splendid, more like an elegant country house. There were rows and rows of very smart metal enclosures. Everything was of the very best. It was mind-boggling, almost like a city. Harvey was in business with a man who was in oil, and seemingly, expense was no problem. There was nothing in Nova Scotia to touch this outfit. Harvey was a delightful chap. He took me around, pointing out what to look for in the breed. It was rather like being in a cow candy-shop, there were so many to choose from.

My mind boggled when I was shown the best animals. They were absolutely huge, as was their cost. In no time flat I found myself buying ten-thousand-dollar models. I bought six. I even sold one of my cars, a saloon Mercedes—which, fortunately, I didn't miss, as I had two, plus a Rolls and a Lincoln Continental—in order to buy two more cows. I came home jubilant.

Having joined the Expensive Cow Club, I began to go to auctions across the continent. When one gets into expensive cows, the whole scene changes. No longer is it just feed and de-poop—it becomes elegant-party time. Take, for example, the Rockefeller sale—it was wonderfully glamorous and exciting. I had arranged to meet Harvey, his wife and another couple in New York to travel together and visit the Rockefellers' first production sale. It was "by invitation only." There was an incredible pre-sale party at what was called "The Party House," on the Rockefeller estate, just outside New York. There was every form of party requirement. Super band, huge swimming pool, a games room. The grounds were lovely, the ballroom elegant, and the food excellent. This was the way to farm. Peggy Rockefeller was also a Simmental enthusiast and her husband, like mine, was a financier. We got along tremendously well. When I asked him about his interest in the cows, he fondly and proudly smiled at his wife and told me that he was only the one who paid the bills.

The next day the sale was held at one of Peggy's farms. There was almost an army of security guards. Everyone was checked and rechecked, and I began to wonder if we were mistakenly about to enter Fort Knox. We were met at the farm gates by antique carriages and driven in great style to the house and farm buildings. The farmhouse was very lovely, like a French castle. It was built of stone, with many turrets and courtyards. The stables were so gleaming that one could have eaten one's lunch off the floor. The day of the sale there was a splendid buffet, and a minstrel wandered around the courtyard singing as we looked over the animals. What a way to shop!

After another elegant meal served with fine wines, the sale began. One very tall, handsome chap reminded me of John Wayne. This was Ed Creed, a farming neighbour of Peggy's who also had a splendid herd of Simmentals. Bless his heart, he supported her in the very first bidding by purchasing half a cow. Incredibly enough, he paid about thirty thousand dollars for his half of the cow. I couldn't help wondering which end he bought, the half that ate or the half that pooped. He laughed when I enquired and said that with his luck it would be the half that did the eating.

The event was a great success. The spirit of the whole thing was wonderful. We were all eager to support Peggy's efforts, and the bidding was fast and furious. I bought two wonderful young female yearlings, which thankfully didn't cost quite as must as Ed Creed's animal. Furthermore I got both ends of each critter.

There were the top breeders from all over the States and Canada and some from Europe. When one sells the very best cows in the world, there is of course a world market, and it is very glamorous. Who says cows aren't classy?

The next day it was on to another farm, up the Hudson River, Ed Creed's farm, in fact. It was another very splendid place. We stayed at a lovely small village along the Hudson. My travelling companions had also bought animals, and the mood was very festive. We were all happy that Peggy was so delighted with her first auction. Again, there was another of those pre-sale parties, this time at a very pretty Old World pub. Nobody parties like cowboys and cowgirls, I guarantee. I had forgotten to pre-book the hotel and so was accommodated in the annexe, a lovely old house a couple of streets away.

At about two in the morning, I decided it was time to leave the party and go to bed. We had to be up early for the sale the next day. One of the men with whom I was travelling very kindly offered to see me back to my room. It was a wonderful night, warm and balmy. My escort had had his full share of hospitality, and it was with great giggles and laughs that we strolled down the moonlit street, ending up at the splendid annexe.

There was no reception desk, just a wide corridor with the rooms leading off of it. Courteous to a fault, my escort insisted on seeing me to the door of my room, at the end of the downstairs hall. Once there, I opened the bedroom door and turned to thank him for his kindness. He bowed, turned and headed glassy-eyed for the front door to return to the main hotel. As I started to show him out and head him in the right direction up the street, we heard my bedroom door slam shut.

"What a nuisance," I said, "my key is on the inside." Without uttering a word, my kind and courteous (if totally sozzled) escort moseyed back down the corridor, removed his ten-gallon hat and, before you could say "manure pile," took a charging leap at my door. He landed against it with his strong shoulder and—Dear God—went straight through it with a crash that resounded in the silence of the night. I stood, frozen with horror, my mouth open. He bowed, replaced and tipped his ten-gallon hat, said, "Evening Ma'am," and made his way back, weaving, like a ship in full sail, from side to side along the wide corridor. Without a backward look, he opened the front door and disappeared, leaving me alone, incapable of movement, gawking at the place where, seconds ago, had been a beautiful antique door, but where now lay a heap of splintered wood. Heavens above! In all of my wildest days no-one had ever actually broken down my bedroom door!

After the terrific crash there was what I can only describe as a deafening silence. I just stood absolutely still, waiting for doors to open and people to shout. I was totally panic stricken. Then, when nothing happened, I collected the bits together and stacked them up. I couldn't possibly go to bed. In a state of terror I sat on the bed wondering what on earth to do. Finally I did a terrible thing. At 5:00 a.m. I picked up my things and left. I just couldn't stay in that room. I walked back down the road to the main hotel, where I later joined my group for breakfast. My mind in a whirl, I mentioned to one of the pals what had happened. It wasn't long before the whole place knew, and soon all of the party-goers of the night before were hysterical with laughter at the incident, especially as my Sir Galahad didn't even remember his noble deed. "Handsome Jack" was a bit preoccupied with his hangover. I think they still pull his leg to this day.

Back at Ed Creed's farm we had another wonderful time, and I bought a beautiful deep-red gal. (She was a seven-and-a-half-"thou" model.) Then it was time for home.

FARM HELP

When I returned home from my first cow-buying sprees and assorted adventures, I eagerly awaited the arrival of my expensive purchases. With the prices I had paid, I could have stocked pretty well all of the farms in Nova Scotia with beef. There was great bustling around the barn to see that everything was perfect for our royal newcomers, whose lineage rivalled that of HM QE II herself, with all due respect. It wasn't that I felt any different towards the new critters than to the herd I already had because they had cost a small fortune. Let's face it, an animal is an animal. I love them whatever their lineage, shape, colour or breed. I have to admit, however, that the "big-buck" factor did creep in, and it came out in the extra sprucing up of their quarters.

Arrival day came for the critters I had bought out west, but they did not appear. Day followed day, and still the new critters did not appear. After three weeks I began to get very concerned. Admittedly Calgary was a long way away, but three weeks' travelling time was surely enough. I began to trace their journey by telephone across the country. Eventually I found out that they were only a few miles from my farm and indeed had been for the last twenty-four hours. Upon investigation I discovered that they had been left in a huge truck on the side of the road, the excuse being that the driver couldn't find my farm. He had apparently forgotten that he had the farm telephone number.

I was absolutely furious when I eventually reached the driver by telephone in a café. He got the message loud and clear that he had better get up off his rear end and get the cows delivered on the double, or an irate farming gal would be out riding the range with a shotgun. Less than half an hour after receiving my telephone call, he arrived with the Royals.

I was too angry to speak. I simply stood at the back of the huge trailer and waited for him to open the doors. When he did so, I just could not believe my eyes. What a state they were in! To say they were filthy, dejected and wild was an understatement. In fact, they were in a dangerous state. An upset one-ton critter is not something to play around with. Thus there were great to-doings getting them unloaded. We had to erect barriers on either side of the truck to be sure that the unloaded critters would go directly into the barn.

When the time came to open the trailer doors, the cows were so frantic that they almost exploded into the barn. The tranquillity of good husbandry was torn asunder with their arrival—once inside the barn, they just about tore the place apart. Enormous though they were, they could jump like deer … the biggest deer you have ever seen. We got the first huge cow into a box stall, where I assumed she would be safe. Thus it was a bit of a shock when she sailed past my ears in the leap of the century. "Dear God," I thought, "it must surely be part kangaroo."

It took hours to get them calmed down and properly housed and tended to. When one critter gets upset, it affects all of them, and all hell is likely to break loose again.

I decided that, come what may, this ongoing rodeo was ludicrous. So I set about, in the next days and weeks, to tame them. I was given the hint that patience and perseverance was the only way, and so I spent considerable time on the end of a rope, being flicked from one side of the barn to the other. As the days went by, my poor battered body went all the colours of the rainbow. My new charges certainly didn't like wearing halters, and they were strong enough to let me know it, but I was hanged if I would be beaten. Being nearly killed was one thing, but being beaten was quite another. So it was that I developed muscles like Popeye the Sailorman's and without even opening a single tin of spinach. But T.L.C. pays off, and in the end, tamed my darlings were.

It was an entirely different matter when Peggy Rockefeller's animals arrived; a splendid and smart cattle truck pulled up in the barnyard. It was super and clean, and the animals were in immaculate condition. Having had the recent experience of the animals arriving from out west, I was absolutely delighted with what Peggy sent. I wanted to hug her. She really cared about her animals, and they echoed her standards of elegance and excellence! They walked off the truck calmly and joined their new family as if they belonged to the place, and I immediately telephoned Peggy to express my appreciation. She was delighted to hear that her critters had arrived safe and sound.

By now Timmy and his pretty wife had moved on, and I had begun to hire help. I called the first of these by the title "Manager," but this soon deteriorated to "Man" or "Lad." I discovered first that farm help is a transient thing, and second that I just don't have the knack for employing people—especially men. I don't think that I am expressly a woman's libber. There is no doubt, though, that women don't stand a chance in this Canadian world of men. Certainly women employing men is an uphill job, rather like trying to carry a sack of lead to the top of Mount Everest. Why, I ask myself, do we women find it necessary to be tough or strong? Why can't things be done impersonally? I got into the habit of stopping, before I asked for anything to be done, to consider the "easiest" way of putting my request so as not to ruffle male feathers, which was ridiculous to me but the most expedient way I could think of.

I soon discovered the things I have going against me as an employer of men. First, I have always believed that men are the strong ones and shouldn't need to be told what to do. Second, I had assumed that when a man looks for a job, he will perforce be at least competent at the job he is hoping to get. On top of these beliefs and assumptions I found it hard to be demanding. I didn't use strong language in arguments, and I preferred asking to telling. Finally, I could do just about every job myself (except for mechanical repairs) and knew just how long it should take and what was possibly the easiest way of getting it done, and that from past bitter experience, so it was impossible to pull the wool over my eyes. Last but not least, I am a soft touch for a sob story. In other words, I am lost from the word "go." Lost perhaps, but never daunted. Never? Well, hardly ever (shades of Gilbert and Sullivan).

To my great sadness I found that it was just not possible to be a buddy or a co-worker or a pal with my employees. This was unfortunate, because living in close proximity, in a pretty remote area, it seemed sensible and preferable to me to be on a more casual basis. Yet it simply didn't work. My teeth would grind when whining voices would give petty excuses for idleness or drunken bouts. God, that would drive me crazy—particularly remaining silent about my thoughts. I had to learn to say as little as possible, and the less I said the more angry I was.

One winter when I was "in between" help, I remember spending Christmas Day on the tractor, trying to snow-plough my way out to reach the rest of the world before finally calling it a day just before midnight—missing Christmas completely. I then struggled my way into January, battling the critters and the weather. On January 4th there was a sudden thaw. As the Girls had been cooped up in the barn for many days, I decided to let them out. Unfortunately I forgot to switch on the electric fence. As they jostled their way joyfully out of the barn, thrilled to be free, they came to the fence and—whoopee!—didn't get zapped. So through it they charged and straight up to their beloved mum's garden.

Now, I happen to be a very enthusiastic gardener, and my very soul screamed out as my Girls, two thousand pounds each of them, cavorted around my lawn, a lawn on which I had spent a summer's back-breaking labour laying turf, de-rocking, fertilizing and goodness knows what.

There they were, frolicking about with gay abandon, each frolic making four more foot-deep holes in my tenderly tended lawn. Screaming like a banshee, I chased them in ever-increasing circles around the house. Finally, voice gone, I sat down on a step and sobbed. A drizzling rain started. I sobbed and sobbed my eyes almost out. The garden was a shambles! The two dogs (mine and one I was looking after) came over, tails wagging, to lick my tears away. In between sobs I told them how completely useless they were, pointed out to them that dogs were supposed to be man's (or woman's) best friend and that the very least they could have done was to bite one of those damned cows. "Look at you," I sobbed repeatedly as those tails wagged at me, "you're just useless."

Eventually, totally exhausted, I picked myself up and went wearily down to the barn. With exhaustion came sanity. I realized how stupid I had been to chase the Gals around the house when all I had to do was produce a bucket of grain. Raving dementia had prevented this sane thought from crossing my mind as I had been wildly tearing around.

I filled a bucket with grain and from the door of the barn called up to the joyous revellers: "Hoy, din-dins!" Presto! The happy high-kicks stopped in mid-kick at the sight of that magic bucket, then—the Charge of the Light Bovine Brigade. In no time flat they, and I, were all back in the barn, the doors firmly closed.

As strength came back, so did the sobs. The Girls cowered from me as I informed them of their impending fate at hamburger junction. Finally, realizing what a total twit I was, I pulled myself together and handed out a generous portion of grain, signifying that all was forgiven.

Back to the topic at hand: farm help. Two friends had been married out by the swimming pool, and after the wedding festivities I had gone away so that the happy duo could have the place for the weekend. I had invited the farm lad to join in the party afterwards and had not given any further instructions. It was a weekend in summer, and I hoped that nothing urgent would happen. When I got back, my pals had already left, and as I was entering the house, I passed the lad, who was coming out of it loaded up with booze. "Naughty," I thought to myself. We had all had our skins full to overflowing at the time of the wedding and to come back for more, uninvited, seemed one over the mark. However, I decided not to make an issue of it, as he hadn't been there more than a few weeks. I was even dumb enough to be embarrassed for him when he dropped one of the bottles he was helping himself to. "I'll pick it up," I said curtly, putting the broken pieces into a plastic garbage bag.

When, later that week, after I had suggested two or three times that the garbage be taken down to the road for collection and nothing had been done, I lifted the bag myself and swung it into the back of my car. Alas, I had forgotten about the broken glass, and as the bag swung past my thigh, it sliced it open—ooooh! A seven-inch cut opened up on my thigh. As I looked at it, the flesh curled back almost to the bone. I stared for a fraction of a second in horror, blood pouring down my leg into my boot, before I clamped my fingers on either side of the cut and squelched my way to the telephone to call the lad and get him to drive me to the doctor. Upon seeing me with blood streaming down into my boots, he kindly offered to patch me up himself. I clutched my bleeding leg protectively, horrified at the thought. "Thank you, but no," I replied and proceeded to beg to be taken to the doctor.

In short, he was a very pleasant lad, but his fortes in life seemed to be playing guitar and drinking, neither of which is a lot of use to cows. Actually, they do like music. In fact, they are very sensitive to music. Being their surrogate mum, I liked to think that they were most discerning in their musical appreciation. For example, they loved for me to sing to them, or at least they seemed to. You see, my Girls wouldn't stand for anything they didn't like. They would even occasionally attack a drunken barn helper, for which I could only bless them, and since they didn't attempt to physically attack me whilst I was singing, I took this as an indication of appreciation.

If I was doing a job and possibly singing a little tune, in the barn or out in the field, they would come over and rub up against me. Of course my heart glowed with love, and I would sing to them. "Shall We Dance," from the musical "The King and I," was a favourite, and I think they knew "The Sound of Music" note for note.

After these concerts, as at so many other times, they would come for a "love of scratchings." It was no wonder my beautifully manicured fingernails gradually deteriorated into black stubs. Bleach became my best friend. If I was attempting to make myself look like a human being, I would just dip my finger ends into the bleach—very soon I worked out just how long I could leave my fingers in the stuff before the flesh actually fell off. Diamonds are most certainly a girl's best friend, but bleach is a close second.

Another of my failures in farm management was a very delightful lad whose dad also loved to come and help. To say the dad was a bit of a pill is an understatement—he was a total pain, always boasting how clever he was at just about everything. I had to learn to close my ears and come up with the occasional "Oh, really?" By now I had learned that the line of least resistance was the best approach. I must say, the lad put up with his dreary dad splendidly. Had I been in his position, I would have personally bopped him on the snout, dad or no dad. But as he was always around, we both got into the habit of putting up with him.

One winter we had really bad freeze-ups in the barn, and even at the house. An icy gale was blowing when, late one evening, I discovered a problem at my main house. No water was coming up, either to the house or to the barn, from our supply down by the lake. This was very serious, and in spite of the lateness of the hour and the weather conditions, the lad and I had to see to it.

Eager to assist in the matter came, of course, Dad. He arrived when I was down inside the water source, a long circular cement tube about four feet across called a crock. The crock was about ten feet deep, with a valve at the bottom attached to the water pipe. The water pipe was in a double casing, so that if anything went wrong, the pipe itself could be drawn out and replaced. Daunted, I discovered that the supply had frozen between the crock and the house. It was so bitterly cold out that every few minutes I had to go indoors to recover and unfreeze myself. When Dad arrived, he insisted I come up out of the crock, where by now I had hung a light bulb powered via several extension cords from the house. Gratefully I obeyed and climbed out of the crock. He went down and immediately broke the bulb. "What a clumsy twit," I thought rather ungraciously to myself.

Well, that was no great problem. I went back to the house and got another bulb. When I returned, to my horror, I saw that he had a blowtorch and was using its flame on the pipe to try to defrost it. Now, this was something that even I knew you never do, because the sudden fierce heat against the icy cold pipe will most certainly burst it. The gale blew my voice away as I bellowed down the crock for him to stop. I was too late—we had a burst pipe. This was another problem we could have done without, but it was not the end of the world. Indeed, it was a damned and cold nuisance but not the actual end of the world, I told myself. After all, he was doing his best.

I knew we had lots more of the piping, way across the field, in the barn. I asked the pair of them to get it, and off they went. Later back they came, empty-handed. Neither of them had been able to find the pipe, so off I set to get it myself. Dragging the huge mass of pipe across the snow-piled fields in the driving gale was a hellish job, but somehow I managed. We just had enough, thank goodness, to cover the distance required.

Unfortunately it's not always possible to keep your eyes at both ends of a job at the same time, and I was a second or two too late to stop Dad's next disaster. The new pipe had been placed within the outer casing and needed to be connected to the pipe near the pump in the basement of the house. They had to meet exactly, which meant that the pipe had to be measured exactly. I entered the pump room just in time to see that Dad was about to cut off the pipe too short. Just as I opened my mouth to say "Don't," he did. Eager to impress us with how clever he was, the idiot had cut the damned thing too short, and we didn't even have a connector to patch it up again. What good would it have done to complain? He was certainly doing his best. Now we were stuck with a splendid new piece of pipe a foot too short to meet its mate. There could be heard the sound of gritting teeth—mine!

However, we had learned to look on the bright side. At least we were now indoors, in the basement of the house, and not out in the driving icy gale. After several telephone calls (by now it was 2 a.m.) it was all credit to a chap in the village that he kindly got up out of bed and gave us connectors. There was the minor aggravation of having to drive several miles into the village to get them, but indeed they were got. By dawn we were back in the water business once again, and the critters could be watered. At least I was spared heaving goodness knows how many buckets of water across fields piled high with snow.

Another time, Dad helped out when there was a problem

with a sliding door in the house. He had popped in with a
pal, and upon learning of the problem, to impress his pal,
he promptly yanked the door out of its groove. I was
astonished! What a stupid thing to do. Need I mention that
he couldn't put it back? Then he just left it there, and later
I had to get someone else to come around and fit it back
where it should have been. I lectured myself that the good
intention was there, but given certain conditions, it is so
difficult to listen to oneself. Alas, I found it impossible to tell
the particular pain in question that I didn't want his help
because he was a travelling disaster. Perhaps I had to admit
to occasionally being a travelling disaster myself, but however grateful I might usually be for help, please, oh please,
not from Dad!

On one occasion the farm lad employed at the time was
approaching his twenty-first birthday party, and he didn't
have his own car. Thus, instead of trading our old farm truck
in for a new one, I decided to give it to him for his birthday.
I'm very "into" birthdays; I could recall my own twenty-first
birthday, and how I would have given my back teeth for a
car, so it was rather fun that I could give someone what I
would have wanted at that age. I thought it would make his
day. Well, it certainly did. He was thrilled to get "wheels"
and, from that day on, hardly did another stroke of work. I
was in fact the hand of my own disaster. That was a lesson
well learned and another rule for the book—don't hand
out wheels.

MACCULLOCH

Every cattle farmer's pride and joy is his, or her, bull, the herdsire. It is from the bull that the herd is upgraded. If you use a poor bull, you get a poor herd. In the Simmental breed a good herdsire should have mighty shoulders, a strong true body, a straight back and a meaty rear end. Not a huge rear end, a meaty one.

A really good Simmental bull can weigh almost three thousand pounds, and that is a lot of bull. The herdsire has to be changed every three years or so, because of the offspring. He can't breed his own progeny. A.I. (artificial insemination) allows the breeder to mix and match in order to get the right cow with the right bull. If a cow is weak in a particular trait, and a bull can be found that is strong in that trait, the two can be matched to produce better calves.

When I began breeding Simmentals, I purchased what I thought was a full-blood bull from the government test station in Nappan, Nova Scotia. It was two years later that I discovered he was only a pure-bred bull and that, as a result, some five years of breeding had been wasted. I was pretty miffed, but it was the Government's first year in its test station, and so the error had to be forgiven. The difference between full-blood and pure-bred is intriguing and is one reason why I became interested in the Simmental breed. It

is possible to upgrade from any kind of cow and get a sort
of hybrid. It goes this way. If you use a mixed-breed cow
which you happen to like because you think she is a good
beef animal, you can breed her to either a pure-bred or full-
blood bull, and her calf will be a one-half pure-bred Simmental. If that calf happens to be a heifer (a female) and
again is bred to either a pure-bred bull or a full-blood bull,
then its calf becomes a three-quarter pure-bred Simmental.
Again, if that animal happens to be a cow and is bred to a
pure-bred or full-blood Simmental, the calf is a seven-
eighths Simmental. If that seven-eighths calf is a female, it
is considered to be pure-bred. You have to go one stage
further with a male, before he, at fifteen-sixteenths, becomes a pure-bred. Upgrading is a great idea because it
enables a farmer who cannot afford an expensive full-blood
to get into the breed by using A.I. The Government does a
good job of assisting such farmers with the A.I. program.

The full-bloods are full-bloods, and one never breeds a
full-blood cow with anything other than a full-blood bull.
Like the kings and queens of England, you can trace full-
blood ancestry way back. Breeding and the various lineages
become a mania with Simmental breeders. Certain bulls
become superstars, and their names are recognized around
the world. My stock became of this standard; my first female
full-bloods were sired by a bull called Fame, who was world-
renowned. I was as proud of my critters as any breeder. After
discovering that my first bull, although he was very splendid
and produced fantastic calves, was only pure-bred, I had to
sell and replace him. He was bought by a very nice man and
went on to a life of bliss with about thirty new wives, so I
don't suppose he had any complaints.

Meanwhile, I had bred some of my full-blood females by
A.I., and one of my best girls produced the most incredible
bull calf. At birth he weighed 110 pounds, which is an
excellent weight, not too heavy. By three months of age he
weighed 440 pounds and showed signs of being a spectacu-

A lot of bull. Young James showing MacCulloch the Mighty.

lar animal. At ten months he weighed almost one thousand pounds. He became a champion before he was a year old, earning his first red ribbon at the premier show in the province, the Atlantic Winter Fair. Even better, he produced female calves and had a wonderful gentle temperament. Some bulls tend to produce bull calves and some female calves … MacCulloch the Mighty, as I had named him, gave us girls, bless his huge heart.

MacCulloch the Mighty was pure gold in every way, adored by his surrogate mother and his concubines alike and admired by every visitor to the farm, whether farmer or not. He had that certain something that sets a champion apart. When he was led by the halter, his majestic walk was something to behold. It was slow and measured, even when he was very young, as if he knew he was going to be huge. There were never any problems with him—he was "right" from the word go. He learned to walk with a halter without any upsets. Quite often when one is training a young animal to walk in a straight line, led by a rope, all hell breaks loose, or they just refuse to move. There was none of this with MacCulloch. When we showed him at the Atlantic Winter Fair, the judge rightly said that there was nothing to touch him, and my heart glowed with pride, especially as he was "home-bred." He walked around the showring as if he knew he belonged there. His mother was huge yet with very fine, elegant lines. She reminded me of a racehorse. I suppose every excellent animal has that same aura of class.

Breeding Simmentals is rather like collecting fine paintings. They are the best, and it is exciting to have the very best. Simmentals are what is called an exotic breed, as are Rolls Royce and Charolais, but my fancy happened to be Simmental. I like Simmental people. It could be my imagination, but there is a sort of link between people who breed them. Indeed we all belong to the Simmental Association just to prove it.

SADIE

Sadie was my Jersey cow. Whereas the Simmental is a beef animal, huge, meaty and strong, the Jersey is bred for its milk, which is high in cream. Simmental beauties are enormous, anything up to almost three thousand pounds of hamburger heaven; the Jersey breed, on the other hand, is fine-boned, delicate and slim, with large soulful brown eyes and the kind of eyelashes that I have always longed to have.

When looking for a milk cow for the farm, I had searched for many weeks before finding Sadie. No-one wants to part with a good milk producer. I found her on a rather remote farm. The old farmer had about eighty cows in his herd and was loath to part with any of them. It took me the longest time to persuade him to sell her to me. I had to promise him repeatedly that I would take the greatest care of her and give her a good home before he would agree to sell. She cost a thousand dollars. She was a yearling at the time and had a wonderful Bambi look about her, so delicate and gentle. When the time came to have her bred, which was when she was about eighteen months old, I very carefully selected her the finest mate I could find. He was a bull from New Zealand. The A.I. man came with the semen, which had been imported especially. Poor young Sadie, she didn't have too wild a sexual fling, that's for sure. I felt awfully

Sadie was my Jersey cow, with large soulful brown eyes and the kind of eyelashes I have always longed to have.

mean about that; it seemed very unfair to her. However, after the usual nine months' gestation, she produced a wonderful female calf, which had markings unusual for a Jersey calf. She looked as if someone had dropped the pepper pot on her—so she was called Pepper.

Our Sadie was a gal of very impressive blood lines, another Royal of the first order. Inspired with this knowledge, I decided now that she was producing milk, we would show her at the Atlantic Winter Fair, the biggest fair in Nova Scotia. Bursting with pride, I set about finding out what I needed to know about showing a milk cow.

Wowzers! I had an awful lot to learn about the art of showing, I can tell you. It was aggravation of every kind. For starters, when one is showing a dairy animal, one must wear white. Not a big problem in itself. The real aggravation begins when one learns that the person playing nanny to the prospective champ must walk backwards while leading the animal around the showring. Rather like ballroom dancing, except that one is never sure whether one's partner is going to waltz, tango or take off for the nearest exit dragging Nanny with her. Add to this the complication that one's partner is much larger than oneself and likely to poop in mid-fling, and the whole thing becomes quite crazy. But if you are determined to show the world how splendid your Jersey cow is, you don't argue, you just follow the rules.

At the beginning there is all of the boring stuff of applying for entry, filling out forms, obtaining certificates and getting the veterinary checks done. When you have successfully waded through all of that hassle, there is the grooming of the future star to contend with.

The grooming starts long before you leave the barn for the fairground. I discovered that Sadie had to be shampooed and clipped, just as any other beauty queen. This was very serious stuff. A neighbouring farmer, Elsie, who had her own herd of splendid milk and cream producers, kindly agreed to come and do the clipping. Clipping is the bovine equivalent of a trip to the beauty parlour. Elsie was a very keen Jersey gal, and seemingly every hair was of the utmost importance. It took hours for Sadie to be primped to perfection. I did the shampooing. I gave it my all, and it wasn't clear who got shampooed more, Sadie or me. It was bubbles, bubbles everywhere. I gave thanks that this sort of business didn't have to be done twice weekly. After the bubbles she had to be rinsed and then blown dry. Yes, even cows have hair dryers these days. When she was dry and suitably gleaming, she was loaded on to the truck and driven away to the fair. I was to follow later.

It didn't occur to me to check up on things, I was still in the "assuming" stages of my farming career: assuming that everyone knew their stuff; assuming that if there were any problems, I would be told. So I didn't cross-examine the lad who was helping with the showing—did he have the required "whites," had he taken all the necessary things for Sadie's few days' stay at the fair … foolishly I assumed he knew the ropes. Another lesson was about to be learned … but then I suppose we all learn; only it takes some of us more time and entails a lot more punishment.

When I got to the fairground, I was pretty damned mad to discover that our tack box had been left behind. Tack boxes are wooden crates into which are packed the grooming requisites for the animals and, most importantly, the rum for partying. Apart from not having the tack box, we also did not have the shovels and other de-pooping utensils. Worse was to come. The lad hadn't brought any whites. I just couldn't believe it. Even I knew that rule. Why hadn't he told me that he didn't have whites? I was absolutely furious. All this way, all the preparation and aggro and now this. How could Sadie be shown if he had no whites? Well, we hadn't got this far to be stopped for want of a few whites. Fuming, I got back into my car and drove back to the farm. Come what may, Sadie was going to be shown.

The whites I had back at the farm consisted of an elegant

Sweet . . . Swee-hee-heet Sadie. All primped up and ready for the fair.

outfit made of French lace, with quite a few frills, and white high-heeled shoes. But so what—whites were whites, and nothing was too good for our superstar. There was no way I would let this situation beat me. Sadie was going into that showring come hell or high water. I had learned one more very important lesson: always check and re-check everything and everybody, and don't complain if you haven't done just that ... yourself!

Upon returning to the show grounds, I had to take the quickest cram course known to man or beast in the art of showing an animal. I had to learn, very quickly, how to lead Sadie. Fortunately she wasn't being shown until the following day, so I spent my time practising with her.

By now we were settled down in the allotted place. Each farmer exhibiting was given a certain amount of space, in parallel lines down the length of the huge building, creating corridors lined with animals on either side. It was all hustle and bustle as we farmers got ourselves settled in, putting down deep piles of straw for our animals. It was interesting that one hardly ever saw poop at the fair. It was whisked away just as soon as it was produced—which was often and in great amounts.

The tack boxes were neatly set at the rear of each stall to be either sat upon or opened when necessary. After each animal was brought into the building and settled down, it was walked around the fairground by the proud owner or exhibitor. As I had never led a cow before and didn't know whether Sadie would, perhaps, set off at a gallop, I practised leading her up and down and around the other farmers' stalls, where animals were resting or chewing or pooping, to get her used to noises and unusual happenings. Whilst I was practising the stops, I would chat with the other farmers— oh my, what fun it was. I would call out, "Look at this wonderful cow, boys, you don't have a chance," and they would laugh and shout their comments back. How I enjoyed myself; I was really "of the land" now.

Later in the day, as evening drew nigh, the stops became longer as I was offered the occasional rum from various tack boxes. It's actually not allowed to keep rum in one's tack box, but hidden with a coke, who's to know? My, oh my, did we party! Many of the farmers actually camp out there for the stay at the fairgrounds; others bring trailers along.

It was a wonderful experience. We were all a happy family, and I was moved to see how the other farmers tended their animals with such devotion. I had soulmates. I felt a very strong bond with them. It truly is a noble calling, being a farmer; it is nothing less than selfless dedication to a very hard way of life. In my opinion, farmers should be paid a million a month—nothing less. I was so happy trudging up and down, around and about, with Sadie's halter in my hand, as she walked delicately along behind. I felt a pang of sadness for city dwellers, who could never know the joy of the tending and caring that we all shared at the fair.

Late at night, after several strong coffees, I drove home, only to return at dawn to get Sadie ready for her class. She was in a class with about twenty others of the same breed, which included my neighbour Elsie and one of her cows. Many of the farmers I had struck up friendships with came to the ringside to cheer me on, bless them, and I was delighted with their support. Why, it was nothing less than back to show biz again! Not only was Sadie gleaming and resplendent with her posh hairdo, but so was I. I was Cow Show Person Extraordinaire—no cow was going to outdo me! So into the showring we both went, with me leading Sadie full steam ahead, backwards!

In hindsight, perhaps it was a bit dicey wearing high heels whilst staggering backwards around a showring in a foot of sawdust. But it was too late to worry about that now. Glamour must pay its price. As I set off, tottering precariously, I was still terrified that Sadie might take off on me. She had never gone through this before (and, as a matter of interest, neither had I), so anything was liable to happen. I staggered determinedly around, holding on to Sadie's halter, telling her all the while how beautiful she was and asking her to please be a good girl for Nanny, or Mummy—she could take her choice. I gave her the occasional kiss on the nose … very soon she looked like a large relative of Rudolph the Red Nosed Reindeer. On we plodded, around and around, with me staggering backwards to the cheers of the crowd in the gallery.

As this was taking place, I happened to catch a glimpse of Elsie and her critter across the circle, and I got a shock— heavens, there was such a desperate look of concentration on Elsie's face. It quite startled me. Obviously it was a matter of life and death to her how her animal did in the show. Suddenly I felt a pang of sadness, coupled with a wave of relief … sadness that the whole crazy event mattered so much to Elsie that it took the fun out of it for her, and relief that I didn't, in fact, care a hoot how Sadie did. To me she was a queen, the very best in the whole wide world. Who really cared about anyone else's opinion?

I decided there and then that Sadie and I would have fun. I truly couldn't have cared less if Sadie had kicked up her heels and danced the Highland Fling with the odd drop of Swan Lake thrown in—to me she was the Champ. I gave her a really big smashing kiss on the nose, and on we joyously plodded and tottered, me still backwards of course and now singing gaily to my Bovine Beauty, to the tune of "Sweet Rosie O'Grady": "Sweet, Swee-hee-heet Sadie, my beautiful Girl." There wasn't a finer, more beautiful cow in the whole world.

Oops ... I got a jolt when my merry song was interrupted by the judge, who was at my shoulder. The Big Guy himself. Someone to be viewed as being only one notch lower than God. Now I know that we (the competitors) were not allowed to speak to judges—just not allowed—so I was totally surprised when he actually spoke to me. "What is Mrs. MacCulloch doing here?" the kindly voice enquired. I vaguely recognized him as a chap I had had a fleeting conversation with at a cocktail party, but I was horrified that he actually spoke to me. "Go away," I commanded rudely, "I can't speak to you. You're a judge." (As if that was a disreputable thing to be.) What a twit I was. The poor chap was only being friendly. It just shows how this showing nonsense gets to one. I had quite unnecessarily insulted him, and he turned away with a hurt and puzzled expression. Onwards Sadie and I plodded and tottered—Sadie forwards, me still backwards and slightly less gleaming white than when I had started out. However, I was still upright, high heels and all.

I then noticed that the judge was waving his walking stick in the air. He had gone over to Elsie, and she then left the circle and went to the spot he had pointed to. Well, that was interesting. She was looking a lot happier, so I assumed he was saying nice things about her beastie. I was both delighted and relieved. I did so want her to win, because it meant so much to her. Then I noticed that the judge was waving his stick at me. Maybe I had been forgiven for my rudeness. I smiled and waved back and continued on around the ring, giving Sadie another smacking great kiss. There was a lot of shouting at ringside but it was unintelligible, and I was concentrating on the waltz-cum-tango that Sadie and I were involved in. Suddenly I heard the chap who was leading the cow behind us calling out to me. I looked around, and he motioned for me to go over to where the judge was pointing. WOT? Seemingly we had got a prize! My joy knew no bounds. I almost burst with delight and completely forgot about going over to the "spot." I threw my arms around Sadie's neck, kissing her nose and hugging her over and over again. The farmers' cheering thrilled me to bits. I was so busy waving to the crowd and blowing kisses to them and re-kissing Sadie that it was quite some time before we got into the required line.

Oh, the bliss of success! Never was there a more delighted duo. As we eventually left the showring, me clutching a ribbon, I led Sadie—frontwards by now, thank you very much—over to the judge to thank him for the award. Sadly, he was still miffed with my rudeness and said gruffly that if she hadn't deserved the prize, she wouldn't have got it. Fair enough, though I was sincerely sorry for being so rude.

Oh, what celebrations followed. You would have thought we had won the whole thing. And, oh my, how we tucked into the hooch. Much later, exhausted but triumphant, The Girl of the Day was loaded into the farm truck and given a well-earned bucket of feed. I still clasped the ribbon "we" had won, singing yet more improvised versions of "Sweet, Swee-hee-hee-heet Sadie." Admittedly my elegant French white-lace outfit was a bit shitty, but so what? My darlings, shit makes roses grow!

CUTLER

Cutler, as I have mentioned, was what I call a "Lassie-type" dog, with the allotted eight miles of nose, incredible fur ruff around the neck and a splendidly elegant attitude. His nose was so long he always seemed to be looking down it, which completely belied his real personality. His tail was the tail of tails—it had a language all its own. You could tell what was going on in Cutler's mind by his tail. If he was pleased, it would wave gently to and fro, as when I told him I loved him, and that he was my "best boy." When he was delighted, it would wag madly to and fro almost wagging itself off. On the very rare occasion he did something amiss, it would hide tucked underneath him, and if he was listening to an interesting sound, it would become tense. When he was setting off an unwelcome visitor, it would be straight out parallel to his back. No-one tangled with Cutler when his tail was straight ... oh no! Truly it was a poetic tail and the dearest in the world to me.

Cutler loved to go everywhere with me. He would always ride on the back seat when I drove about in the Rolls Royce. As we travelled, I would glance into the rear-view mirror and see him sitting there, looking elegantly and with great dignity out of the window. "My darling," I would say to him, "you do look so splendid." This he would acknowledge with the blink of an eye. He reminded me for all the world of a grand duchess dressed in splendid furs. He was so luxurious-looking and so totally charming. Gentle, unassuming and loyal. How I loved Cutler! He was always there. He never intruded, always adored and was simply a part of my soul.

As the farm was pretty remote, I taught Cutler to tell me if anyone arrived from the shores of the lake. He became very zealous about this task. He was so zealous, in fact, that he didn't wait until anyone landed on our shores but took to shouting in the most abusive manner at every speedboat out for a jaunt. Cutler seemed to think that they had to be informed in no uncertain terms just who was on duty around the place. He had amazing long-distance sight and could spot them long before I ever could, when they were still a mere dot in the distance.

It was whilst Cutler was on faithful guard duty that he discovered his singing voice. It was a very still evening. As Cutler took his nightly stroll along the shores of the lake, near the house, attending to his self-imposed rounds, he must have thought he espied one of those intruders far across the lake. He immediately gave a great wooooooof! I couldn't see anyone around, but as I looked, I heard a second woof that didn't belong to Cutler; it was his echo.

The reaction the echo had on Cutler was a riot. He jumped a full foot off the ground. He obviously thought that there was a huge dog behind him. As it was a lovely evening, I was practising my putting on the putting-green at the side of the house by the lakeshore. I started to giggle, and putting down my putter, I went over to him. Sitting on the sandy lakeshore, I put my arms around his neck and gave him a big hug. "It's your own echo, you twit," I told him. Delighted to be hugged, he gave me a very special tailwag. But instead of snuggling in close for yet more hugs, as he usually did, he pulled away, looking in every direction for the terrible beast that had just insulted him with that monster wooooof. In vain I told him that there truly weren't

"Shall we dance?" Cutler's cue for our favourite game.

any monsters around except for him, but seemingly that echo had to be put in its place—so he began shouting at it. Every time he gave a mighty woof, back would come another woof, which had to be woofed back at. Cutler woofed, his echo woofed, Cutler woofed back, his echo woofed back … this, to Cutler, was total warfare. After a while I gave up trying to tell him it was his echo and left, still giggling, to let him get on with it. It was time to do the evening's barn and critter chores. Cutler and his echo went out of my mind.

Later in the evening, after dinner, Cutler followed me into the music room. I played the piano for a while and then said to him, "Shall we dance?" This was his cue for a game we played, which went to the tune of "Shall We Dance." I would hop, singing, around the music room—field, beach, or wherever we happened to be at the time—and he would dance around me, barking. We both loved this game.

Usually I would put out my arms and start with "Shaaall wee" … and before I got to the word "dance," he would join me with barks and jumps, all up and down and around me.

On this occasion, whilst hopping up and down and around the music room with me, the only sounds to come out of him were hoarse little squeaks, not a single loud splendid woof was to be heard. It seemed Cutler had lost his voice from shouting at himself! I collapsed from my dance in helpless laughter, hugging him and telling him that if he shouted at himself all day, he could not expect to sing at night. I don't think he was too distressed about the lack of voice, he was just too busy loving all of those hugs.

From then on, if life got a bit dull, Cutler would amuse himself by going down to the lake and shouting at his echo. Nothing I could tell him would induce him to accept that there wasn't really a bad guy lurking around, one with a very big woooof! Whenever he came back to the house barkless, with only a hoarse croak, I knew he had been telling his echo a thing or two.

T.C. BUCKITT
A DOLLAR OR A BUCK

All my life I had loved animals but had usually owned dogs, rather than cats. I think it could fairly be said that I was basically not a cat person. They kill for the joy of it, and I hate that.

One day I was visiting a farmer's wife. We were chatting in the kitchen whilst she bustled about getting coffee ready. As we talked, I heard a sound from behind the kitchen door. Without thinking, I got up and opened it. Out shot a tiny black-and-white kitten. "Oh, what a sweet little thing," I exclaimed, picking it up. Although no cat person, I would never be cruel to one. I won't gush over them, cooing "Pussy, oh, Pussy" and all that stuff, but a baby of any sort is special, and this one was no exception.

As I held it gently, stroking its fur, I was quite startled by the reaction of the gal with whom I was having coffee. "Oh, is that thing still around?" she said, frowning with annoyance. "It was supposed to be hit over the head this morning." "What?" I asked, horrified. "We can't find a home for it, and we have too many cats around here as it is," she said. "But you can't hit the little thing over the head just because you don't want it," I protested in horror. It hadn't asked to be born! The thought of a sweet, innocent little creature being clubbed to death was just appalling. How could anyone even contemplate such a thing? Without a second's hesitation, I acted.

"I'll take it," I said as I handed over a dollar for purchase of the tiny creature. "I don't want payment for it," she replied. "No," I said, "it's bad luck not to pay for it." Finishing off my coffee, I rose to leave. The farmer's wife found a cardboard box, put the kitten into it and tied a string around the box. Then I said my goodbyes, left the house, got into the car and drove off, having put the box on to the seat next to me. On the way home in the car, there were scrabblings and clawings in the box, and eventually the little creature managed to get out. This didn't worry me, because she certainly wasn't going anywhere. All the car windows were closed, so I just let her play a game of discovery. She roamed around the car, full of curiosity and quite fearless. When she had finished discovering, she came to sit on my shoulder. I was amused at how fearless she was as she took in the scenery—while singing loudly into my ear—all the way home. Need I relate that by the time we got back to the farm, I had fallen in love with this tiny bundle of black-and-white fluff. Motherhood had spread. I was now the cat's mother, as well as the cows'.

For the first few days I decided to keep her indoors so that she could become familiar with her new home ... know her roots, so to speak. She slept on my pillow, and there are no prizes for guessing who didn't get any sleep. She was so happy with this arrangement that she sang all night long, with one paw outstretched to occasionally pat my face. There was no real wonder that she was happy (who wouldn't be) to be out of that basement and away from the danger of being bashed on the head? I was terrified that I would turn over in my sleep and crush her, so I got no sleep.

She was the dearest of creatures with the deepest of purrs, bless her heart. To my surprise she had no fear whatsoever of the dog, who in his turn thought he had been given another baby to love. He developed an immediate posses-

My Dollar Princess. She was the dearest of creatures with the deepest of purrs.

sive love of the little thing, and they started a wonderful friendship. Oh, the fights they had, with the kitten hanging around the dog's neck like a necklace, hacking away at the eight-mile-long nose. It was lovely to watch. He was so incredibly gentle with her that if one of those sharp little claws hit their mark, he would only whimper and retire to a corner of the room until he forgot about it. Sometimes, when she overdid the clawing, he would give one of his very loud barks, which would almost frighten the life out of her, and she would run up a curtain, out of reach. I called my latest critter Dollar Princess because I had paid a dollar for her. I thought it was a splendid name, and it suited her.

She obviously loved her home and her pal Cutler, and indeed her surrogate mum. She would follow me down to the barn and play nearby while I did the chores. When I went around the fields checking various things, she would follow tirelessly, and when the grass got too long, she still came. She would find her way through the grass by taking tremendous leaps, with all four legs splaying out. In mid-air she would look quickly around to find out where she was. Having thus gotten her bearings, she would continue her pursuit. If, during a walk, she got tired, she would often rush up a tree and howl, or she would throw herself down on the ground on her back, legs in the air, until I picked her up and put her on my shoulder. There she would ride, singing loudly. She was total enchantment, and I was a converted cat lover.

A few months later she began howling very loudly outside the barn. I assumed that she had now matured and was calling for a mate, and so I telephoned the vet to make arrangements to have her spayed. I was informed that she had to stay in overnight and that I would be able to pick her up the next day, when she had recovered from the anaesthetic.

After dropping Dollar Princess off at the vet's, I returned home, did the evening's chores and had an early night. The following morning, at dawn, I came sleepily down to the kitchen to have a snack before going down to the barn. For a change I had had a good night's sleep, without Dollar Princess. I put a couple of slices of bread into the toaster, then turned away to fill the kettle with water. Sleepily, I smelled a strange smell. "What could it be?" I wondered. Then I heard scrabbling sounds and turned in time to see little hands trying to get out of the top of the toaster. I screamed, pulled the plug out of the toaster and shot like a bullet to the other end of the house. I was by now very much awake.

It took the longest time for me to persuade myself to go back to the kitchen. I would die, I was certain, if anything was still scrabbling in the toaster. Gingerly, I opened the kitchen door. There was no sound. With the greatest of efforts, I made myself walk over to where the toaster was. No sound. "Oh, God!!! Please let it be gone," I prayed. Somehow, I made myself look down into the toaster ... there was something dark down in the bottom! For the longest time

I actually couldn't move. Then, at last, I managed to pick the toaster up and open the bottom. Out fell the poor little mouse, totally toasted; not just rare or medium but frazzled completely, its poor little backbone burnt to a crisp. I was ill! "Oh, God," I moaned, "I toasted a mouse!"

My fit of the horrors was interrupted by the harsh ringing of the telephone. It was the vet. "We've got a problem," he said. "He has a problem," I thought to myself. "Wait until he hears what my problem is!" Mouse massacre! Then I thought of Dollar Princess, and my heart skipped a beat. Oh heavens, what could be wrong? All sorts of terrible things flashed through my mind. Aren't we supposed to have only one major tragedy a day? "What is the problem?" I asked. "It's a male," said the vet. WOT? Our delightful Dollar Princess was a feller! It seemed that I was such a super farmerette that I couldn't tell a he-cat from a she-cat. "But she hasn't got a tassel," I protested. Young bulls all have "tassels" (private parts) mid-way between their front and back legs, and I hadn't seen any sign of a tassel on Dollar Princess. "The plumbing is all at the blunt end," the vet informed me. It appeared that he-cats weren't endowed with the same plumbing gadgets as he-cows. "Well," I said, giving the matter due consideration, "you'd better chop off the bits we don't want, and I'll come and pick it up."

Later that day I picked up the critter from the vet's surgery. "It" was still dozy with the anaesthetic. After placing it gently upon the cushion I had in the passenger seat beside me, I drove home. My mind was full steam ahead. What on earth would I call it now? I couldn't call it Dollar Princess, because it was certainly no princess—it was an ex-feller. So I changed "Dollar" to "Buck" and, taking into consideration the recent surgery, changed "Princess" to a simple "it." Our Dollar Princess became Buckitt with a stroke of the knife.

After Buckitt got over the surgery, it came to life with a vengeance. Nothing was safe from that cat's boundless energy. During the night, when it decided it was playtime, it was playtime. This was all well and good whilst the novelty lasted. But enough was enough, even for a loving surrogate mum. There is nothing more guaranteed to wake the sleeping dead than a needle-sharp claw stuck into an exposed foot. I would waken with a howl and, without thinking, grab the mini-monster and hurl it to the other side of the bedroom. Oops! So much for motherly love. Now, being flung across the room might intimidate any ordinary cat, but not Buckitt. He loved this game. Being hurled across the room was the signal to Buckitt that the party was just beginning. Back he would bounce, ready for the next fun.

Another "fun" thing I discovered was that I have a small black mole between my shoulder and my neck. Buckitt thought it was something that needed to be attacked and would proceed to do just that in the middle of the night when I was fast asleep. I can tell you that I was just delighted when Buckitt discovered the barn. And from then on, that was where he spent his nights.

Love Buckitt though I did, I was disgusted at the gifts he presented me with. These were dead or half-dead creatures of every description. One night, hearing Buckitt yelling by the kitchen door, I went sleepily downstairs to let him in and trudged back up to bed. Some time later I was wakened by scrabblings and chasings around the bedroom. My mind cleared instantly—Buckitt was chasing something in the bedroom! For a while I was paralysed with horror, then I got out of bed and tried to rescue whatever it was. No luck. Eventually I had to go back to bed, and at last whatever it was was caught—by which time I was trying hard not to be sick. The last straw was the crunchings coming from under the bed; that was just too much. I gave up my bed for that night, preferring to sleep in the music room downstairs. The midnight feast could go on without me.

On another occasion we had an unwelcome visitor in the kitchen. From the signs, it was another mouse, who, with the cold weather coming on, had come in for warmth and

After surgery Buckitt came to life with a vengeance.

shelter. As a polite hint, I set down every kind of stuff I could find marked "Scram" and such, but this mouse seemingly couldn't read or was far more interested in other edibles. The situation was a bit ridiculous. We had one fit and murderous cat which daily brought its victims home as love-gifts, and still we had a mouse in the kitchen. Having tried the persuasion techniques and failed, I had to result to fisticuffs. Instead of letting Buckitt out one night, I decided to keep him in. He could do his stuff in the kitchen instead of the barn.

Needless to say, I couldn't go to sleep that night. I lay awake, listening for developments. In the middle of the night I heard a commotion downstairs. I shot out of bed and went to investigate. As I opened the door, something small and furry whizzed past me and bolted to the other end of the house, into the music room, followed by something large and furry, namely Buckitt. I decided to leave them to it. I retired back to the other end of the house some eighty or so feet away and made myself a hot "cuppa." At what I thought was a suitable time for Buckitt to have disposed of the thing, I went back to investigate. I opened the door to the sound of terrified tiny screams. I could not listen to those tortured sounds, so I ended up rescuing the mouse by throwing Buckitt out of doors. I had learned my lesson. I would just have to put up with the mouse.

Once, I woke to find one of my presents leap-frogging around the bed, trying to escape Buckitt. With a howl, I jumped out of bed, grabbed the cat and threw him out of doors. Whatever it was he had brought in would stay there until morning. That is the one thing I truly hate about cats: their cruelty ... the way they kill for the sheer enjoyment of it. I can't come to terms with that, and the excuse that it's their nature doesn't, as the expression goes, ring my chimes. I loathed Buckitt's presents.

Buckitt took a great liking to the farm lad of the time, who wore blue jeans. At the morning break I would usually make us both coffee in the kitchen, and he would pet Buckitt. Delighted with the attention, Buckitt would run up his blue-jeaned leg, clawing his way up to the shoulder, where he would perch, singing loudly whilst getting his ears rubbed. This was fine with the lad but soon became a problem with other people. Buckitt, used to being the centre of attention, would run up every pair of blue jeans that came into the house. There were some very alarmed people at times, I can tell you. Not everyone wearing blue jeans wanted a black-and-white monster clawing its way up to perch on their shoulders. On top of this Buckitt could pick out anyone who had allergies to cats, and they got his full attention. If a visitor arrived while I was preoccupied making tea or mixing a drink and there was a surprised shriek, I would always know that it was Buckitt doing his thing.

Visiting dogs would sometimes take it upon themselves to sort out Buckitt. It was very amusing to watch the drama unfold. The visitor would chase after Buckitt expecting the cat to take off in fright, but Buckitt was made of sterner stuff. He would hold his ground, ruffle up his fur to make him appear even bigger than he was, and then he would come in for the attack. Oh, the countless dogs I have seen head for the hills after a set-to with Buckitt. Many a time I had to rescue the visiting dog by locking Buckitt in a room to keep the peace. That farm belonged to Buckitt, Cutler and the cows ... no other animal was allowed in Buckitt's book.

Through these escapades, it was not very long before Buckitt got an addition to his name. He got his initials, T.C., after that chap in the television show "Magnum P.I." T.C. Buckitt stands for "Tough Cat" Buckitt, and I'll tell you something for nothing at all ... Buckitts are beautiful!

NEIGHBOURS, WALKIES
AND WATER

I spent one whole summer playing happily at building a new farmhouse, and it was tremendous fun. There was so much to learn about building a house. It was a sort of adventure; every now and then you miss out collecting the two hundred dollars as you pass "Go," but that is to be expected. The kitchen in a farm is possibly the most important room. It seems to be the place where everyone gathers. So I wanted my farm kitchen to be perfect and designed a huge one, twenty-eight feet by seventeen, with a vast fireplace. Apart from the usual things kitchens have, this one had a bar and a sitting area with a chesterfield in front of the fireplace, as well as a breakfast area. It is important to be able to do everything in the farm kitchen, to do it in a wonderful, warm, welcoming atmosphere.

After vainly attempting to explain to the bricklayer how I wanted my hearth, I gave up, and I went off into the fields to collect fieldstones myself. Barrow load by barrow load, I hauled them back to the building site. Then I made a deal with the bricklayer. If he would mix me the mortar, I would play with my own rocks. Well, without fear of contradiction, I think I can say that my farm fireplace turned out to be the bees' whiskers. It is about eight feet wide and ascends all the way up to the ceiling, and the hearth stretches the width of the room. Antique is putting it mildly. It looks as if it came with the flood. I managed to scrounge a very old barn beam about a foot square by eight feet long and got it set across as a mantle with huge pins going all the way through it to the wall. I was very impressed and very content with my new "old" kitchen. Everything about it was just super, and above all, it was psychologically right.

I learned the hard way about water. Take it from me, you've got troubles if you don't have any water, and you've got troubles if you've got too much water. You've got troubles if your water is too soft, and you've definitely got troubles if your water is too hard. I didn't know at the onset of my aquatic adventures that, in fact, you don't need to drill a well. Given the right conditions (and also, of course, water), you can make do with digging a huge hole, and if that hole is higher up the hill than you are, then you get "gravity-fed" water. However, drilling companies are no fools. They aren't going to let you in on that little "wrinkle" until they've made a wage packet or two out of you—and so you struggle along, learning, one hopes, from your mistakes, marking each one up as a part of the game.

I got a very good drilling company and decided I would have it drill my new well inside the garage, so that if anything went wrong, there would be none of that messing around outside, down a bitterly cold crock, in the middle of a freezing dead-of-winter gale. I duly marked the spot with an "X," and they got to work. I was surprised by how quickly they went down. In no time flat they were down to 175 feet, looking for bedrock. I was also surprised to learn that it is in bedrock that you find good water. Alas, they didn't find bedrock but they did hit gyprock—the worst thing you can hit. Gyprock causes the water to be hard and have many problems, and so they came back up about ten feet, and out burst fifty gallons a minute. The stuff gushed everywhere, apparently unstoppable. Oh, would that it had been Texas Tea!

They tried all sorts of things and eventually managed to stay the flow to thirty gallons a minute. The result was that the garage had to be moved sideways so that the well was outside with its ceaseless excess flow, and a channel now had to be dug for the new stream to flow down the hill to join the existing stream.

Although I had all of those gallons of water where many people couldn't get any on their land, the water was dreadful. So, after making do for a while, I decided to try to find better water. I thought I had hit good fortune when I found a water diviner, a local Dutch farmer. It was absolutely fascinating the way he trotted around with a forked twig. He kept stopping and marking the spot. I followed to heel like a faithful dog, believing his every word, as he insisted there was water. Oh yes, I was a believer. What I wasn't aware of was, I was also a sucker. I ordered a huge excavator to come and dig. One place we were instructed to dig was just above the swimming pool, on an upward slope from the house. If we found water there, the house could be gravity fed. Oh, oh, oh, wonderful! My excitement knew no bounds. I was fed up with hard water. The man with the big digger got digging!

We had almost got to Australia when our Dutchman had to concede that, probably, the water was indeed down in Australia. So we filled the first huge hole in (it was about thirty feet deep and wide) and moved a hundred yards further up the hill. Again the digging started, and back to Australia we headed. When we had matched the first hole in depth and size and hadn't found a drop, we filled it in. Australia would have to keep the water. I telephoned the Dutchman and told him of our lack of success, and he returned, complete with some huge bags of vegetables, which he told me he grew. I bought the bags of veggies. It was a trade—veggies for more accurate information.

He suggested that we now go down the field about four hundred yards. This dashed the hope of gravity-fed water, but I was determined to get decent water, and so it was back to the digging. We had gone about fifteen feet down when a tiny trickle of water appeared. At the sight of it, the Dutchman guffawed loudly with delight—we'd struck it, we'd struck it, he told us, and off he went, clapping himself on the back and laughing uproariously all the way back to his truck. Odd but different!

By this time a few friends had joined in the fun, and we watched the trickle, which after about five minutes dwindled to nothing. To be sure, we went down another fifteen feet and then decided to call it a day. We would wait until the next day and see how much water appeared in the deep hole. Two days later we had enough water for morning coffee for two, at which point I decided to hell with the idea of digging. We would put up with the water we had for now.

I got a man to bring a machine for treating the water. He arrived in quite a novel manner, landing in his own plane on the lake. You can't get much classier than that, can you? I wondered what the plumber would arrive in, maybe a tank or a jumbo jet? We chatted for a while in the kitchen, and he turned out to be a distant relative. It seemed, furthermore, that my chemical relative had a cottage nearby, and that he too had hard water. He thoroughly understood hard water. In fact, he told me it took forty drops of something or other to change one vial of his water from blue to green (or the other way about). He tested mine by the same method, and it took eighty-four drops to make the change occur. I don't think water comes any harder than that. I bought the machine he recommended to cure the problem.

Still hellbent on good water (because an ex-Brit never gives up), I gave great thought to my situation. Then I had a brainwave. In the course of my search, I had learned that sand was a great conductor of water and a purifier. Well, at the side of our stream, which never froze in winter, there was a large area of sand. Perfect! I couldn't wait to get that digger back and start digging another hole.

It was a bit more tricky this time because the walls, being sandy, kept collapsing. So instead of getting one deep hole into which a cement crock, about four feet in diameter, could be positioned so that we needn't head yet again towards Australia (which from my standpoint appears to have cornered the market on good water), we had to make do with a very wide, shallow hole into which we set three crocks in a group. After they were put into place, the sand was replaced until only the tops of the crocks could be seen. I was very proud of my master-plan, which included a channel dug across to the stream about four feet deep and filled with gravel. The next day, Heaven be praised, all of the crocks were filled with water. I could hardly believe my eyes. I had done it! Joy of joys, at last we would have soft water. Surely this time I had gone past Go.

Alas, no, I was not allowed to go past Go, because I didn't know as much as I thought I knew. I didn't take into account the fact that the manure, which was piled up at the back of the barn, was uphill of the water crocks we had put into the sand. It wasn't very long before that splendid sand had filtered the barn poop slap and slurp into the new well, and we were getting molten poop out of the tap. Not good. In fact, not good at all! The stench was terrible! However, having become accustomed to adversity, I still didn't give up. A girl of quality and charm never gives up. I thought things out really well again and decided to go upstream, higher up than the barn. Surely nothing could pollute the water up there, apart from the odd deer or porcupine.

Back came the digger chap. He was beginning to feel quite at home, he said. Power was mine; I was getting bigger and better at water wells. This time we had four crocks and three whole truckloads of rocks to put around them. We should end up with a reservoir sufficient for a small town and there it was—at last, at last, wonderful, clear, soft water. It was a dream come true. Until the frost, when it all froze solid. A less-hassled mortal may have been disheartened, but do recall that I had been through the mill a few times by now, and having come so far, I was not about to give up. Not deterred in the slightest, I simply switched back to the original hard water from the drilled well. At least I had learned one thing, not to burn my bridges. I hadn't got rid of the first pump. I felt really smug when, at the freeze-up, I could merely switch from one pump to another. Hard water was better than no water at all. Further aquatic endeavours would have to wait until the spring. For now, I was weary of water problems. I put on a pretty dress and gave a party; champagne is preferable to water any day.

One day at the new farm I was wakened at about five o'clock in the morning by a loud banging at the kitchen door, then a man's voice shouting angrily. I got out of bed sleepily and looked out the bedroom window. Down below was a chap with a bald, very angry head yelling up at me. He was the closest neighbour. He lived in a cottage about a mile or so down the road, and my Girls, seemingly, were chewing up his garden. I didn't lose a second. I grabbed my frilly housecoat and put it on over my really flimsy nightie. I ran down the stairs and out the door. He was still yelling away, quite red in the face. Heavens, my Girls might be the death of him! He wasn't the least bit appreciative of my leaping out of bed at that hour to listen to his tale of woe, nor of the fact that I was out of the house and heading towards the truck at the speed of sound. This mother cared about her children.

As I shut the truck door behind me, my frilly lace housecoat caught in the door. Through the window, I heard my neighbour shouting that I couldn't do any good on my own. If that was so, why was he bashing on my door at 5 a.m., I wondered. "Little do you know, buster," I thought to myself. Leaving him still yelling, I drove away, my frills flapping from the truck door in the pre-dawn breeze.

As morning was just breaking, I spotted the Girls near the neighbour's cottage and brought the truck to a stop. Although they were near his cottage, they weren't in the dreary garden, which he was still so passionately shouting about. You'd think he would have been grateful for the free manure but not a bit. His car pulled in after my truck, and he followed me, calling out unwanted advice, as I tripped with gay abandon into the dewy field.

Strange as it probably looked—a gal in a nightie, equipped with nothing but a large diamond, dashing into the middle of a hay field at dawn as the mists were rising—that was the scene he got, like it or not. "Now, darlings," I reproached the Girls, "you really are so naughty. What are you all doing here?" It was pointless to join in the loud yelling, it would only frighten the Girls, who knew anyway that they shouldn't have been there. Kate, my pet, came over to me immediately for a hug and a few loving scratches. Seeing Mother's pet getting all of those scratches, more of them came pushing in to get their love and scratches too. Having got all of their attention I called, "OK, Girls, it's time for walkies. We're going home." Bringing the scratchings to a halt, I set off calling "Hup ... Hup ... Hup" across the field in the direction of the barn. Bless their dear hearts, as I hupped and clapped my hands, they lifted up their heads and followed me across that field towards home. I wanted to hug them all, I was so proud of them!

To give the chap with the angry red bald head his money's worth, I sang and danced along to "We're off to see the wizard, the wonderful wizard of Oz." And not alone— my Girls danced with me; they tossed up their heels and we all cavorted our way back to the barn. I, for my part, did not need to do morning aerobics that day.

Later on that year, when I ran out of pasture, a land-owning neighbour said I could graze the Girls on his pasture. Grateful for his offer, I put a halter on Kate, my huge dark-red pet, who habitually bullied the rest of them. Although Kate was very affectionate towards me, she was pretty awful to all of the other animals. She ruled the barn dwellers, and I caught her many a time standing squarely in the barn doorway refusing to budge to allow the others to pass in or out. The rain could be beating down or the snow falling by the megaton, but there Kate would remain, showing them who was boss. With Queen Kate leading the way, the Royal procession trudged its way in splendid style to the new pastures. We passed our red-faced friend's place with total disdain, heads held high; it was on to bigger and better pastures.

They stayed there for a week and then, alas, brought themselves home. Thank the Lord they didn't call in at my bald neighbour's cottage on the way. I found them one morning outside the kitchen door, along with a lot of poop. I decided I could hardly scold them for coming back to Mother, so I led them down to the barn, calling "Hup, hup," gave them more grain and put them back into a field. They would have to be taken back later in the day because we just didn't have enough grass left on our pastures.

Later that afternoon I once again put the halter on Kate, and we set off down that yellow brick road ... but the Girls had spotted my wonderful green lawn as we set off, and no way would they follow Kate and I. Up into the garden they gleefully charged. "Hoi!" I bellowed. "Come along, we're going walkies."

Oh no, they weren't, they were going gardenies. I tied Kate to a tree (which she bitterly resented) and chased the rest of them around the house, screaming my head off. Every joyous leap churned four more holes out of my beautiful garden. I was blind with rage. Around and around the garden we thundered. It really was quite ridiculous. On about the fourth tour, I noticed the young herdsire, Mac-Culloch—a beastie of some three thousand pounds—contentedly rubbing himself up against one of the four pillars outside the front door. During one luxurious monster rub against the pillar, it went crashing down! "Oh God, they're pushing the house down!" I shrieked to no-one in particu-

lar—there was no-one else there. I was about to rush over
and bash him on the head when I heard a splash behind me.

I turned quickly to see that a young calf had fallen into
the swimming pool. I found myself rooted to the spot—I
didn't know which way to run. Was I to rush over and bop
MacCulloch on the nose (which he probably wouldn't feel
anyway), or was I to rush to the aid of the young calf? The
dilemma solved itself very quickly when I noticed that the
calf had kicked and splashed its way to the deep end and was
disappearing beneath its own waves. Without hesitation, I
jumped, fully clothed, into the pool. In mid-leap, I realized
that I couldn't open my eyes under water.

As I, too, disappeared beneath the waves, I had the
presence of mind to feel around. By good luck I caught an
ear and hung onto it like grim death. In spite of the calf
kicking and struggling madly, I managed to tow it to the
shallow end, where I discovered yet another problem—I
couldn't lift it out of the pool. The damned thing was too
heavy. I had four damaged discs from a riding accident and
was hopeless at bending and heaving. I had to think quickly.
The calf was in a great panic, and the huge Mums had now
gathered around the shallow end, making gentle, encouraging cooing noises, whilst the rest contented themselves by
eating my flowers. My rage returned with a vengeance. "I'll
give you cooing," I bellowed at them. "For ten cents, you'll
all be hamburgers by morning." By way of reply they pooped
all over the patio, whilst I coped with the flaying feet of the
terrified calf.

A sudden fear caught me: perhaps the calf would give
itself a heart attack out of panic and tension. Then I broke
up with laughter. "Dear God," I said to myself, "what am I
worrying about? If anyone is going to have a heart attack
around here, it's going to be me."

Ever the improviser, I towed the calf over to the metal
step-ladder. I managed to wedge its two hind hooves on to
the lowest step, then got its two front hooves on to the top

steps. Whilst supporting its back with one hand, I bobbed down under the water, got my shoulder under its rear end and gave a mighty hurl. Olé! The thing catapulted out of the pool. Over to it dashed all of the Mums with wonderful motherly love, but they scattered in great fear and haste as I climbed out of the pool and began yelling at them and waving my arms like the avenging angel. Then there was the usual stampede down to the barn, where eventually they did get their grain. I was too weary at this point in the game to think of punishment. They would stay at home until I got my energy back to take them once again down the lane. This Pied Piper of cows had had enough of Bovine Beauties for one day.

THE NUT

Being a farmer has been many things. Apart from being damned hard work, it has been interesting, puzzling, horrifying, fascinating and certainly different. Perhaps being both a widow and a farmer has made my experience a little more tricky than others'. I don't know, but I have become involved in some quite extraordinary conversations. Dealing with them has oft-times been like walking a tightrope. One has to make split-second decisions as to how to react, in order to best deal with the given situation.

An example, concerning Pal Pete (who is certainly one of the kindest men on earth, a person who would never knowingly be cruel or rude or ever be offensive), was when he had called around while I was doing the evening barn chores. He was leaning over a rail in the barn having just had a nip out of his rum bottle. Pete is not averse to the odd drop of rum. As I heaved the bales of hay and spread them out for my Girls, we chatted about the pros and cons of the critters. The day's work finally finished, Pete followed me up to the house and into the kitchen, where I lit the fire in the big stone hearth in the kitchen. Although the fireplace looked as if it had been there for a thousand years, it was built, as I mentioned, with my own fair hands. I am what is called "into" stonework. After a hard day's labour a cheerful relaxing fire is a splendid thing.

Pete had had a head start at bottle and was wont to be in a meditative mood. As I began preparing dinner (I usually eat late, possibly because I'm European, unlike most Canadians, who eat about 5:30, which is the middle of the afternoon for me), he sat at the kitchen bar reminiscing about his recent stay in hospital. Usually our conversations would begin with what he had done that day with his dozer. (Pete was a dozer operator, and he was one of the best at this line of work.) This evening I was preoccupied with a problem I was having with one of my calves and was only half listening to Pete, who in a pleasant conversational manner was discussing his "Nut." For the longest time I assumed the Nut was something to do with his machinery. With my mind elsewhere, I naturally associated this Nut problem with his dozer. I was still thinking about the calf when yoiks ... I realized that the Nut in question was a personal appendage. I almost passed out. But what could I say then ... seeing that we were well into the conversation. I couldn't very well barge into those deep meditative thoughts with sudden outrage and yell, "I don't want to discuss such a thing!" That would be ridiculous. Conversationally, it would seem, I was stuck with the Nut.

How to deal with the embarrassing situation went whizzing around in my brain. Pete meanwhile, gazing sadly down into his drink, chatted on. This Nut was obviously serious stuff. It seems he had narrowly missed a fate worse than death during his recent hospital stay, when he had almost come in for surgery on that (for him) dreaded Nut. This Nut was apparently something to which he was not only physically but emotionally attached. Speaking almost to himself, he continued to gaze down into the depths of his drink. Who was I to disturb such deep meditation? The Nut had the floor.

Turning suddenly towards me, he held up one of his huge fists ... "Big as that," he stated sadly. Supplying a response created a problem for me. Not having been tuned into the conversation from the beginning, I still hadn't got the gist of it. So I wasn't sure whether to congratulate or commiserate. To tell the truth, I wasn't too sure exactly what the Nut was. It could have been one of several things, and I didn't wish to upset or offend as it appeared to be a serious problem. So I picked up my drink and sipped it, letting silence speak. Pete continued: "And I just don't have the nerve to go and get it seen to." I made a quick decision. I would treat it as casually as if we were discussing the weather. Brightly, *en passant,* I enquired, "What do you think they would do? Would they cut it off, do you think?" This had an electrifying effect on Pete, who almost fell off the bar stool upon which he was precariously perched. Ooops, too late I realized that I had said the wrong thing. This Nut was obviously something sacred, and not a thing to be chopped off lightly.

Still not exactly sure of what that Nut was, because I had never heard of anyone's personal parts being called by that name, I broached it from a different angle, kindly suggesting that if it was a problem, maybe he would be better off without it. Mollified that perhaps things weren't all that desperate, he settled back to gazing into his drink. "You're right there," he agreed. Relieved, I said, "Well, there you are." I still did not know what on earth I was talking about but was convinced that I must change the subject to something cheerful and uplifting. Whatever this Nut was, it was filling the place with gloom and despair. "Isn't the new calf wonderful?" I asked. "Do you know it weighed over 130 pounds?" A delighted smile spread over the sad face. "Did it now?" he said, the Nut immediately forgotten.

Breathing a silent sigh of relief that the offending Nut had been laid to rest, we chatted pleasantly about the new arrival. I will, however, never be able to look at a squirrel again without thinking of dear Pal Pete—especially if it's eating a nut.

THE BIRTHDAY PARTY

As I have already mentioned, my birthday falls on St. Valentine's Day. You'll notice the year was omitted—ladies don't ever tell their age—suffice to say that I am working my way back to twenty-one.

My friends are all delightful and elegant people in their different ways. Many are doctors, perhaps because I had at one wild stage in my life a yen to be a brain surgeon ... (maybe there is a God of Mercy after all—I never made it). Some are what could be called "of money," some have successfully made it for themselves, and some don't have it and aren't interested in it, other than putting bread and wine on the table. But we all have one thing in common: we love to dress up and party. We Brits don't talk about our friends' status in life; it's not considered the thing to do, unless for a specific reason. It goes without saying that it would be sacrilege not to dress elegantly and formally for our parties. I am convinced that if one makes the effort to look either splendid or fun for an occasion, one automatically enjoys oneself more.

Thinking of my doctor friends (many of whom are vets), it amuses me to remember that it takes longer to be a vet than a doctor. I recall a fun pal I had years ago in England who was a vet. I took my cat to him for treatment one morning whilst myself suffering from a doozy of a hangover. The disgustingly cheerful pal saw instantly that I was not in the best of sorts and chatted brightly about my saddened condition. I recall asking him to hurry up and sort the cat out or he would have Body Number Two to worry about, namely me. He handed me several multivitamin tablets and commanded me to swallow them with a glass of juice. To my amazement I felt great within ten minutes. To this day, whenever I'm under the weather, I think to myself, "I'm not feeling too good; I think I'll call the vet."

Back to the party. This was a perfect Valentine's Day. Glistening snow lay by the ton outdoors. The sky was a spectacular blue, and the sun was blindingly bright across the landscape. Who could want a prettier birthday? Well, the weather was one thing, the conditions quite another— I mean, the conditions in the barn. The chap who was supposed to be helping me on the farm hadn't bothered to arrive, so I had started out my birthday morning dressed in heavy-weather gear for mucking out the barn and tending to the cows. I had about sixty of them at the time. As dawn broke, I was singing "Happy Birthday to Me," digging my way down to the barn, with Cutler, my dog, at my heels. The snow was piled four feet deep, and by the time I had dug my way to the barn, I was exhausted and hot. So I just lay down in the deep snow, looked up at the sky and sang another chorus of "Happy Birthday to Me." Cutler loved this and jumped all over me, tail wagging, licking my face for his happy birthday.

When my strength returned, I heaved myself to my feet and went into the barn, where my heart sank as I discovered that one side of the barn's water supply was frozen solid. This meant that all of the gadgets which were supposed to automatically refill with water as the animals drank were now solid ice.

"Wouldn't this just happen on my birthday," I thought, and since the wretched lad hadn't turned up for work, there was no alternative but to start heaving large buckets of water from the sink tap (which thankfully was still working) to the animals. I was determined to have a happy birthday, and so, to fight off the unenviable task I was about to begin, I started a sort of game, because I refused to not enjoy every minute of my birthday. As I brought each critter its water, I sang it a song and scratched the name of the animal and its song on a barn timber with a nail. As I sang, I was trying to sort out which critters I could put where, to effect the minimum of heaving. It was like playing musical Bovine Chess with four-footed moving parts. There was great jostling to get at the water, so I had to isolate each one from the rest, let it drink its fill, then write down it and its song before letting it loose. Each watered Gal had her tune. I reckon they drank about three huge buckets each. Heavens, I was almost dead by the time that little exercise was over. And almost out of songs after singing sixty of them. It was a wonderful moment when I passed a bucket around and not one was interested—they were all happily chewing away at their hay, and that was the sound of music itself!

I managed to get things unfrozen with an electric kettle and, straightening out an aching back, left the barn. Then came the struggle back up to the house through the deep drifts of snow, which the wind had blown into the channel I had dug earlier that morning. It seemed a lifetime since I had got out of bed. When I at last got back to the house, I shed all of my poopy clothing and boots in the walkway outside the kitchen door, then headed straightaway for the bath.

As I soaked in hot, perfumed, bubbly luxury, I decided that I was entitled to put cows and barns out of my mind for at least a short while. It was, after all, the anniversary of my day of birth. I popped open a bottle of champagne and toasted myself—I couldn't think of a better way to re-start the day. As I emerged from the bubbles, the first of the friends arrived, laden with fun gifts, and of course more of that necessary champagne: I do have a great weakness for champagne. In fact, I could cheerfully bathe in the stuff.

Early that evening, having partied for much of the day, I didn't mind one bit having to don the heavy-weather gear and dash down to the barn for the evening feeding and watering session. When one is afloat with champagne, the barn chores don't seem so hard. At least in the evening there was the minimum of de-pooping, that major hassle being done mornings only.

This time the party pals came too, and I've got news for women's libbers: men have definitely got the edge when it comes to heaveho-ing. Having masculine muscles to throw around those heavy bales of hay was treat *numero uno*. When the barn dwellers were attended to, we all struggled cheerfully back up to the house through the snow, throwing snowballs at each other. Then—oh boy!—off came my stinky barn gear for the last time that day, and I dove into the bath for the transformation into party birthday-girl of the evening. Armed with a bottle of champagne, I splashed about in my bubbles ... Oh, this was the life. For this evening I was no longer a farmerette, I was a Valentine.

Whilst I had been de-pooping, some of the gal pals had been busy in the kitchen getting things ready for the birthday bash. Sadly, funds no longer ran to butlers, maids or even cleaners; it was a matter these days of being a one-person army.

All of the party pals took part in cooking the lavish meal. The atmosphere was wonderful; everyone was in formal evening dress and looked tremendous. I think we had just about everything there was to eat in life. It was so good to be in the company of great friends, to eat and drink splendidly and to relax in the soft glow of the candles, set in lovely antique crystal candelabras on the table. There is no doubt that the look of a table makes for elegance as much as the food upon it. And, without doubt, my birthday party was elegant.

The *pièce de résistance* was the birthday cake, made by one of the pals, Margot. Margot is not only beautiful but also very artistic, and the birthday cake was devastating, as well as huge and disgustingly creamy and chocolaty—a whole year's diet gone at a glance. Some bright spark had found incredibly tall, thin candles, and the cake was completely covered with them. I pointed out to the gathered throng that I was not, in fact, one thousand years old today, as the candles seemed to indicate. I almost burst my lungs attempting to blow them out, encouraged by outrageous comments and laughter. The fun and rambunctiousness went on full swing. Everyone had so much to say, and so much of it seemed to be said at the same time that the noise of animated chatter and laughter increased continuously, to form a wonderful birthday atmosphere.

After I had blown the candles out and pictures had been taken, we were just tucking into the liqueurs and brandy when the door opened. No-one had knocked or been announced, it just opened. Through it entered my neighbour Pal Pete and his son-in-law, each armed with a large bottle of rum. We were not the only ones in a party mood that night. Pal Pete was a frequent visitor. He loved my cows and often came to the rescue when the farm help let me down. Pete was always welcome even when uninvited.

The dinner guests didn't quite know how to handle the situation. They fell silent. Pal Pete and his buddy were dressed for the woods and probably weren't even the slightest bit interested in how they looked or indeed how anyone looked. A party was a party to our boys. It was more than obvious that they had been at the "wine gums," as both were glassy-eyed and staggering, exuding merriment, fumes and good cheer and certainly ready for more. Accustomed to unusual happenings, I arose from the table to greet them with a welcoming smile. "Hello there, it's my birthday party," I said. "Come and join us." To the stunned, silent gathered throng, I said, "This is Pal Pete." There ensued a bit of confusion as the guests not too keenly shoved their chairs aside and two more were added at the table. Being city people, they were possibly not accustomed to having a couple of pretty wild-looking honchos drop in uninvited, unkempt and soused to the gills to a birthday frolic for which they themselves had donned their best bibs and tuckers. Pal Pete smiled delightedly as he and his pal, oblivious of the furore they were causing, cosily joined the others.

Now, my pal Pete is the salt of the earth, with the heart of a giant—always ready to do anyone a good turn. A good man, notwithstanding the fact that his blood count is probably going on 1,000 percent neat alcohol. Fortunately the birthday candles had already been blown out, because, with the fumes Pete and his buddy were breathing so generously over us all, there might well have been a couple of cases of spontaneous internal combustion.

The birthday cake had been cut and was being passed around. As the cake made its way around the table, I noticed Margot, the gal pal who had made the cake with such artistry, T.L.C. and oceans of cream and goodies. With a face that only Gainsborough could paint, she was watching Pete. Pete, when the plate was passed to him, had ignored the cut pieces and taken the largest uncut piece—about a third of the cake. Now, oblivious of Margot, and of the rapt attention of all of the other guests, he was happily ripping it apart with hands resembling huge sledge hammers.

He then called Cutler over (who, although being allowed anywhere in the house, is never fed at the table) and, whilst laughingly announcing to the throng that he never ate the stuff, fed the ripped-up pieces of cake to the dog, who quite obviously thought he had died and gone to Doggy Heaven. There was eager, if slightly disgusting, slurping and licking as the birthday cake disappeared eager gulp by eager gulp. I am sure that my dog didn't realize that he was taking his life into his own paws, so to speak, by accepting the goodies

The birthday cake.   The smile of the century–Pal Pete.

offered, because Pal Pete almost fell off the chair on top of him a couple of times. The awful doggy eating sounds were the only sounds in the room. Apart from that slurping and gulping and slobbering, there was utter silence. The guests watched transfixed. For my part, I could hardly breathe. I knew that if I did, I would burst with laughter. Heavens, what was going to happen next?

The atmosphere was broken by someone suggesting that more photographs be taken. Pal Pete, bless his heart, seemed to think that it was his bounded duty to be in the dead centre of every picture and proceeded to place himself exactly there, displacing anyone who got in the way with a mighty friendly nudge. Pete, I should mention, is no slip of a guy. He is a tall chap and quite bulky. Combine this with the deadly fumes he spread around him, and you'll see why nobody argued the toss. They obediently made way, and the pictures were taken with Pal Pete full centre stage, smiling a delighted, if somewhat glassy-eyed smile, surrounded by assorted (and certainly different) expressions.

A while later, when it was announced that we were all going on to another party, I thought it was rather sweet that

Pete, in fatherly fashion (whilst managing to hang on to a door jam to prevent himself from falling flat on his face), gave me a piece of fond advice. "Now, you look out for yourself driving," he said. "You've had a lot to drink." A wonderful pal is Pal Pete!

RODNEY

Angels, I can assure you, do come in various shapes and sizes. My angel appeared at my kitchen door one morning at 7:30, when I was lying on the chesterfield with a plaster cast on my left leg up to the knee.

The previous evening I had been invited to a party in the city, nearly an hour's drive away, and friends had arranged to pick me up. After having finished the evening's barn chores, I was crossing the icy barnyard to the house when I fell. I twisted my ankle very badly and proceeded to pass out with the pain.

When I came to, I was desperately cold. Goodness knows how long I had been lying out there in the bitter cold of winter. I tried to get to my feet, but I just couldn't stand up, nevermind walk. The only thing I could do was to crawl on all fours, or rather threes, through the deep snow, back up to the house. This was a matter of a couple of hundred yards, including a small bridge across a stream and up about twenty-four steps. At least the ordeal warmed me up. I had just made it to the house when the friends arrived, and they took me to the city. Once there, they deposited me at the hospital, where I insisted they go on to the party. There was no point in all three of us having a dreary evening.

It was about 11 p.m. by the time I was attended to and ready to be released. I looked most impressive with my monster white-plaster leg. I was instructed not to put any weight on it until the next evening, in order that the plaster could set. I got a taxi and, being a true party girl, went to join my friends. When I arrived, the guests were just leaving, but things soon heated up again, and a good strong drink cheered me up no end. Later my party host and his wife insisted on coming back to the farm with me.

After the last guest had left, they loaded me carefully into their car, and we all returned to the farm. There they kindly insisted on staying the night with me, bless them. Chess, the husband, who was the head of a giant oil company, said that he would feed the critters the following day. The look on his face, however, belied his jovial tone. He was a city person and, unbeknownst to me at the time, quite terrified of the cows. So it was with trepidation that I bedded down on the kitchen chesterfield for the night.

I was in a great deal of pain; in fact, agony. Certainly it was impossible to walk, let alone tend to my Girls. Such was my state when in walked the angel. Rodney was my angel's name. He had heard that I had a problem and had come to help. Well, bless his heart, no-one was more welcome. He was tall (well above six feet off the ground), lean, with a positive shock of long fiery-red curly hair. Under this wild mop were a pair of large blue poppy eyes and slightly protruding teeth, which disappeared into a long, fuzzy, red beard. The Devil himself might have looked good to me at that time, as I lay helpless wondering what I was going to do about feeding and tending to the cows. But Rodney proved every inch an angel. As I started to tell him what needed to be done, he assured me he knew what to do and disappeared. I could hardly believe it. You have never seen a more expressive look on a face than on Chess's when he walked downstairs later that early morning, and I told him that it was OK, there was someone to look after the cows.

The prospect of facing those critters had not been a lovely one for him, and it was a great tribute to him that he was, in spite of his fear of cows, prepared to give it a try. He went off to work in the city a relieved human being, leaving his sweet wife, Ruthie, to care for me for the day.

A while later Ruthie came down for breakfast. I told her the good news of Rodney's arrival, and she set about making coffee. I was lying facing the swimming-pool patio—and got a sudden jolt when a very large, dark-red head silently appeared in front of the patio doors. It was Kate, the pet of the herd.

Kate always came up to the house, fence or no, to let me know when she was upset or if anything was wrong. She was a frightful bully to the other cows, so none of the herd ever dared tangle with her. She was enormous, and she was my baby, rather like a very large red dog that said "Moo," but it was a shock to see her vast head at the patio window. I called out to my friend, "Ruthie darling, I'm afraid you'll have to chase the Girls back to the barn."

Now, I didn't notice at the time because I was only concerned with the cows, but Ruthie almost fainted with fear as she went valiantly to the patio door, opened it and started shooing the Girls back to the barn. It was the funniest sight. Ruthie is a petite gal, and my Gals were very, very large. This was a battle between a 110 pounder and a lot of 2,000 pounders. The odds were not in little Ruthie's favour. Ruthie became sort of rooted to the spot as more and more of the herd appeared with unmistakably worried looks on their faces. They weren't in the least bit intimidated by Ruthie—they ignored the poor girl. One could almost read their thoughts: "What, indeed, is this dot on the horizon?" and "Where is our mum?" I couldn't help it, I started to giggle. It was incredibly funny seeing Ruthie and Kate nose to nose. Between giggles, I shouted at the Girls to shove off back to the barn. My horizontal position just made them all the more curious. They wanted to see where their mum was. Kate almost got into the kitchen, but still valiant, Ruthie did her fierce bit.

"Kate, buzz off!" I bellowed. And then, to Ruthie, "Wave your arms around wildly." Clad in slippers and dressing gown out in the snow, Ruthie did as suggested, whilst I fell about with laughter, and finally managed to get them to go away. Bless her heart, she looked for all the world like an imitation of Don Quixote. Eventually back she came through the patio doors, breathless but triumphant. As she shut the doors firmly behind her, she put her hand to her chest. Then she sat down on the floor and burst into tears. I was absolutely astonished. I had thoroughly enjoyed the whole event, but I just hadn't realized that she was absolutely terrified of cows and hadn't wanted to alarm me by telling me so. What a pal! The valiant sweet soul had faced my huge Girls nose to nose even though she was in mortal fear. She was a good friend!

Having got it out of her system, she made us coffee, and we were just beginning to giggle together about the whole situation when Act Two started and the girls reappeared. This time they were hotly pursued by Rodney, so sweet Ruthie didn't have to risk life and limb again. Over the next day or two things got organized.

Oh, what a character our Rodney turned out to be. He was very likable. Yes, he drank. But then, it seemed to me, who didn't? Oh, and yes, he was great with the singing. Actually the more he drank, the more he sang, and the more he stuttered. It wasn't very long before I could tell the degree of boozery he was into by the level of stutter or the lilt of song. It fascinated me that my Girls loathed him with a passion. I couldn't believe my eyes when, one day, I saw one attack him. They had not done anything like that before! But he didn't even seem to notice it particularly. He took it in stride. He liked the Girls, and who knows, maybe he was accustomed to being attached by cows. He was, all else aside, a wonderfully cheerful chap, and we got along famously.

In March, when the snow was on the ground, Rodney suggested that he burn a field to rid it of dead grass and weeds and provide some nutrient for the soil. I was surprised to think that the field could be burned, even though snow was on the ground. However, Rodney, our man of the land, assured me that he had been an expert on fires since the age of twelve and that it could be done. Who was I to argue with such expertise? Secretly I wondered if I had gotten myself landed with an arsonist, but then there's nothing like a new experience to perk up one's agricultural day.

In spite of all the snow, Rodney managed to get the field on fire, whilst I lay on the kitchen chesterfield cast and all, with my fingers crossed, praying that he wouldn't burn the house down with me in it. But my fears were unfounded. He spent days happily burning everything in sight as I occasionally watched fascinated. (All the while, nevertheless, I secretly prayed that he would continue to spare the house and the barn.) Then he turned his expertise on the woods behind the house. I had a grandstand view of things from close quarters, and it was quite wonderful to see how much could disappear in his fires. I was most impressed, and he was happy as a clam.

As Rodney stayed on, a routine began to come into place. When he got his pay cheque on Fridays, his pals would come to collect him, and they would go off to drink themselves into oblivion. To be helpful, I suggested that I do both the Friday-evening barn chores and the Saturday-morning chores, so that if he overdid the partying, there wouldn't be a problem. He could have fun and not worry about the Girls—my Girls that is, not any of his.

On a particularly clear, sunny Friday, with snow thick on the ground, Rodney got busy with his fire as soon as he had finished the morning barn chores. He had a huge one blazing away in no time flat, and I went out after lunch to join in and help drag things to throw on to the blaze. When his buddies arrived, shortly after 2 p.m., he went off to

change his clothing in preparation for the weekend's partying. While he was gone, one of his buddies came over to join
me by the fire. The buddy's journey was an interesting one
to observe. It was an intricate kind of dance-weave-stagger
which, at one point, threatened to take him straight past me
and into the fire—but at the crucial second he managed to
put in an extra lurch and come to a halt just in front of the
flames. Whew!!!

As he approached, I happened to be downwind of him.
He reeked of booze; in fact, he smelled as if he had been to
bed with the stuff. Now, I don't object to booze, but I'm not
ecstatic about a mixture of stale booze and bad breath, and
that was what came in strength downwind from our friend,
the buddy. Having arrived by the fire, he got himself firmly
planted there, feet apart, which gave me some relief because he still appeared to be in grave danger of falling in. By
some miracle, however, he became reasonably firmly
planted. I watched, mesmerized, as he stood swaying gently
to and fro in the breeze, in a world of his own. I might not
have been there. The sun continued to shine, the sky was a
clear, brilliant blue, the snow was a blinding white, the fire
crackled away, and Buddy swayed.

"Good afternoon," I offered. No response. A short silence, more swaying, and then Buddy took a deep breath,
"So what are ye doing then?" he came up with. "I'm helping
to burn old wood and brush," I answered politely. Long
pause. I waited for something further to happen, starting to
pray that it wouldn't be a fall into the fire. I was concerned
in case any diverting of his concentration might interrupt
the sway, which looked as if it held him together, so I held
off further comment. Buddy took another deep breath and
came up once again with "So what are ye doing then?" In
case I hadn't spoken clearly, or on the off chance that he
had a hearing problem, I raised my voice a bit and repeated,
"I'm burning old wood and brush." No reaction. The
swaying continued as he stared thoughtfully into the fire.

Then he turned suddenly towards his buddy, who hadn't yet approached the fire, and bellowed, "Hey, git over here then." Without waiting for a reply, he stopped in mid-sway, turned directly towards me and said, "My God, yer a limey, you old bitch—and a very nice one too." Stunned silence. My jaw dropped. I was also swaying in the breeze, keeping time with Buddy. Was I going a bit cuckoo? Could that possibly have been a compliment?

Whilst I was beating my befuddled brain for something suitable to say in reply, Rodney reappeared and thankfully took Buddy away. The smell of stale booze and bad breath floated off, and I breathed fresh air again, contemplating my compliment.

I was still contemplating it the next morning when I went to the barn at 7:30 to do the chores. Rodney was already there, singing louder than ever, which was a signal that he had had a merry night. I enquired after his friend, whether had he got home safely. "Oh, ye've no need to worry about him," stated the singer of the century. "When he's sober, there's nuttin he wouldn't do for yer. When he's drunk, he's crazy as a fart." Dear God, what could I say to that. I had a problem: I had never had occasion to discuss the merits of a fart! I could think of nothing to say.

THE RULES OF THE BARN, OR SNEAKINESS

During the winter months the herd stays safe and warm in the barn at night and comes out during the day, weather permitting, for exercise and fresh air while the barn is being cleaned out. From the fall on, the animals are segregated: the calves born that year are separated from their mums, who are by now pregnant with the next spring's calves and need a rest from feeding the ones big enough to be on their own; the mature cows have their own enclosure, as do both sexes of the young. The bull, the herdsire, the king of the farm, has one to himself. Our three-thousand-pound gentle giant, MacCulloch, had his own pen in the corner of the barn, with its own door opening to his outside pen. A bull can be dangerous just because of his enormous strength and size, so his pen has to be very, very strong. Ours was built with four-inch steel bars.

With beef animals, the bull has his fun and frolics during the late spring, fulfilling his mission in life by fathering the youngsters to be born the next spring. After he has done his stuff, he idles around all summer, chewing contentedly alongside his concubines, safeguarding his herd. During the winter he is separated from his family, so as not to allow the young females to be bred when they are too young. Breeding at too young an age can even cause the death of the young female if the calf she is carrying is too big for her to give birth to. The winter separation is very distressing all round, particularly when the youngsters are taken from their mothers. The yelling from all concerned makes life in the barn absolute hell for a week or so, until they get used to the new conditions.

One very hard winter we had blizzard after blizzard, building up walls of snow. Life was one continual drag: digging myself and the herd out of our respective houses, piling up walls of snow in an attempt to get it out of the way and finally getting the animals out into the paddock behind the barn, where they were allowed for their winter exercise. How well I recall spending two whole Christmas days on consecutive years, perched up on the tractor ploughing a path to the animals to feed them and then another to the road. Christmas dinner was a sandwich eaten with frozen fingers in the barn. But, back to the subject of bull, no matter how kind and gentle any bull is, it is foolish to trust him, because it can kill you with even a playful nudge.

A three-thousand-pound affectionate rub is a terrifying thing! Whenever you are in the bull's pen, you have to be sure that you don't get into a dangerous situation, such as trapped between the bull and a wall, in case he does indeed affectionately rub up against you, looking for a scratch. He doesn't know that he could crush you in the process. I always carried a hay fork. Besides its self-defence value, I found it a great way to satisfy his longing for scratchings. I would rub the hay fork carefully against his skin. Oh my, how he loved that treat, and it was a splendid relief to those much-abused fingernails.

Outside, around the top of his pen, ran a strand of wire through which ran an electric current, so that if Mac-Culloch was tempted to try to jump out, his nose would touch it first with a metal ring (usually put in bulls' noses when they reach a year old). The current would give him a smart zap, enough to make him think twice about it. (It's a

MacCulloch the Magnificent with a ring in his nose.

ghastly thing seeing a ring being driven through a young bull's nose, but it's a necessary evil: the nose is the most sensitive part of a bull's anatomy, and the ring makes it possible to control its enormous strength.) I have been zapped by touching an electric-fence wire and can assure you the zap you get is enough to curl your hair—even if you've got a bald head.

On one particular day, after several severe stormy days during which the animals had been cooped up in the barn, I could at long last let them out. With might and majesty, MacCulloch the Magnificent strode out into the sunshine to greet the glorious sparkling day. Strange, isn't it, that after a terrible snow storm, the sky is usually wonderfully blue and the sun extra shiny and bright. MacCulloch was truly a magnificent sight as he pounded the snow down with his front hooves, snorting excitedly. He exuded power and masculinity.

The previous night's snowfall had been very heavy, and as MacCulloch surveyed the world, pounding the snow down into a hard pack, he was quite high up. In fact he looked quite comical, like a very large pea on a gleaming white drum. There he was perched high up on his snow mound, with the top electric wire well below his chest height, rather than where it should have been, at nose height.

Having fed him, and having noted that he was enjoying being out in the sunshine, I didn't pay him much attention. I was now busy clearing the snow from outside the large sliding doors of the barn. I needed to get the tractor out to start yet another bout of snow-ploughing down to the road. The cows at the other side of the barn were pushing and shoving each other as they lined up to get out of their pen door and into the sunlight. Once out, they frisked and frolicked glad to be free and in the sun. To add to the excitement, one of them was "in season," which is an expression to describe that the cow is eager and ready to mate. Poor MacCulloch! His fun and frolics were restricted to his own quarters. It wasn't the time of year that beef animals are bred, which is May-June.

I was so intent upon my task that I wasn't paying particular attention to MacCulloch. Seeing the cows jumping around outside and scenting the one in season, he began to get excited and leaned forward, touching the wire fence. (I had forgotten to turn on the electric-fence switch. Ah well, we all forget something sometime.) Having touched the fence and having not received the expected zap, he knew immediately that he could not be contained. Well, it didn't take this would-be lover long to seize his chance. With a mighty leap "Handsome Charlie" was over that fence!

Ye Gods!!! The awesome power of those three thousand pounds of hamburger flying past my ears with a roar was absolutely terrifying. I shot into the barn and closed the large sliding doors, my heart pounding. I wasn't dumb enough to be brave and risk getting killed in the cause of frustrating true love. "Let the bovine nuptials commence," said I to my terrified self.

Past experience had taught me that MacCulloch's second passion in life, next to making love, was grain. So I dashed to the grain sack, filled a bucket and went to the cow's exit door to show it to him. It must be stated at this point that there is no great courtship or romance in the bull-cow mating game. There is no exciting or romantic leading up to the great event in bovine sexual behaviour. It goes something like this. There is the dashing up to the gal in season, a quick sniff at the rear end, followed by the jumping on to her back, and in seconds, that is it. I mean, if the Gal in question happens to blink her eyes, she would quite possibly miss the event. Anyway, by the time I got to the door of the barn with the bucket of grain, the romance was over. His ardour now quenched, all thoughts of his new bride disappeared at the sight of the bucket, and he kicked up his heels with delight and dashed towards me.

I could almost read his thoughts—"Can this really be true?" must surely have been one of them, or maybe he thought it was his birthday. Two goodies within the space of a few minutes was pretty good going. Anyway, he charged back into the barn, knocking aside all in his way, eager to get at that grain. Being nobody's fool, I quickly put the bucket down and did a sneaky dash around him to close the door from the outside. This was called a "gotcha." Greedily he tucked into the grain ... so much for bovine love. Then, even more sneakily, I opened his inner-pen door and lured him back to his own pen with another bucket of grain, hooked on a hay fork. By doing this, I was able to keep a distance between us both and to get out of the way quickly if need be. I needn't have worried. It was quite amazing how happily he went back to his pen. Nature must have told him that his job was done. As for me, I sat down on a bale of hay and started to shake.

Reaction had begun to set in. It's no mean feat coping with a frightening and potentially dangerous situation when quite alone. After about ten minutes, the "shakes" subsided, that weak feeling of shock faded, and I was able to carry on with the morning's chores. My golly, I had been lucky! Then I had to smile at how super-sneaky I had been. That made at least three of us with smiles on our faces around the place: one of relief and two of fulfilled bovine bliss.

One evening when I was feeding the herd, I noticed that one of the Gals had what looked like thousands of needles sticking out of the end of her nose. I took a closer look. They were, in fact, porcupine quills. There were so many she must have been in agony. As my luck would have it, she was one of the biggest of my Girls, weighing about two thousand pounds. This was going to be a problem. I was alone, and she was a very large critter to tangle with.

I called the vet, and when I told him which cow was involved, he wouldn't come. He knew this gal of old and was bright enough to not risk being crushed to death. The fact was undeniable, this cow was a man-hater. When faced with a man, she was capable of, if not pulling the barn down, at least giving it a fair try. She had been like this ever since a Man from the Ministry had given her an injection when she was pregnant and had frightened her so much that she had tried to leap out of the restraining pen. She got caught halfway over it and lost her calf the next day. From that time on, she had been a very tricky animal to deal with, and to be honest, I shared her dislike of the Man from the Ministry. The event had been quite unnecessary.

Nevertheless, something had to be done. Having first of all closed the barn doors, locking her and a few others inside, I approached her, putting out my hand to give her a loving scratch. I had purposely kept a few other critters with her, so as not to alarm her. As I scratched her and cooed lovingly, I formulated a fiendish plan. It is simply amazing what one can come up with in times of pressure. First I remembered rule number one: don't try to out-muscle them, you'll never win. Then rule number two:

bribery is the "in" thing in the barn, so out came that friend in time of need, the grain bucket. Immediately she pricked up her ears and came towards me—so far so good. I had to dump some grain on to the cement floor, because she couldn't eat out of the bucket with all of the quills sticking out of her nose. She managed to scoop up some of the grain with her long tongue.

Somehow or other I had to deal with the problem of her great strength. On top of the grain I laid two rope halters in a big circle. Then, as she licked up the grain, I managed to get the halters, one at a time, up and over her head. Because she was concentrating upon the grain and trusted me, she didn't mind one bit. (What magical things they are, buckets of grain.) I tied her head at each side to an upright post in the barn, securing her in the centre. Throughout this, I stopped every now and then to scratch her, to keep her content. Then I got to rule number three, the Sneaky Rule. I had prepared a couple of grain sacks by making holes in them and slotting in string, and before she knew what was happening, I had popped these over her eyes to keep her from seeing what I was doing. She had had her fill of grain, and I kept up the scratching from time to time, so she wasn't hostile, just puzzled. Wow. That was an amazingly good start.

She couldn't see me as I crept up on her with my pair of pliers, singled out one particular needle and yanked it out. This done, I shot like a bullet out of reach of those legs and feet. Oh boy, could she leap about! There were legs kicking in all directions, accompanied by agonized howls. I prayed the ropes would hold. When the howling and jumping stopped for a moment, I slipped in and did the next one and then the next. Poor dear, there were so many of them. She was bleeding all over the place by the time I got the last of them out three hours later. It was a good thing I had happened to notice her plight, because after I had calmed her down and let her loose, she went straight to the water container and drank and drank and drank. The poor dear must have had those quills in there for quite some time. Exhausted and having completed my Mission Almost Impossible, I went back up to the house and gave myself a triple gin and a pat on the back.

CALVING TIME

Calving time (any time from January to May for beef animals) is hectic. It is also happy, sad, worrying, relieving and intense, if you care for your critters as most good farmers do. And traumatic as it is to lose a calf, every farmer must expect it sooner or later. I simply can't bear death. Losing a calf devastates me.

One day in calving time, during the evening's barn chores, I noticed that one of the heifers was about to have her first calf. For non-farmers, "heifer" is a term used for a female cow which has not yet given birth to a calf. As with human babies, one is apt to worry more with a first calf. Anything can go wrong, and so extra measures are taken to ensure a safe arrival. One reason birthing problems are more likely with heifers is, because they have not gone through the process before, their birth canal is not yet stretched. Although the gestation period of cows is the same as humans, they don't come out like human babies, but rather like divers, their front hooves first, then the nose and head and then the rest … one hopes. If they don't come out in that order, you've got trouble.

Rodney and I had decided to check up on her every two hours, in shifts. I had the 10:30 p.m. shift. I was a bit concerned because she had been in labour since late afternoon, and so I decided to check her internally, which is a bit gruesome and scary. It took almost super-human courage for me to put on a very long plastic glove (which went all the way up to my armpit) and shove my hand up the blunt end of the mother, where the baby was to come out. I needed to know if the hooves were in the correct position of coming out first. The next check is to see if the nose is following because if the head is turned in the wrong direction, the calf cannot be born; the head has to be turned with nose first before the next birth stage can occur. Simple abnormalities like a turned head can sometimes be turned back around, but it is usually essential to get a vet if it is a breach birth, that is, if the rear end presents itself first. If one is alone and desperate and the calf is the wrong way around, one can only hope to push the calf back in (which requires a huge effort), then grasp the rear hooves and get them out one at a time so that the baby can come out backwards. The procedure is a nightmare for both the farmer and the animal.

This one, however, proved upon inspection to be coming out in the right direction (thank you, God). The only problem seemed to be that it was a big calf. She would need help. I would also need help, as I am not good at pulling because I have a troublesome back. It was bitterly cold in the barn. Expecting a long night, I went back to the house and put on more warm gear, then returned to the barn vigil. By midnight the two hooves had appeared, and Rodney should have been on his way to take over. As I waited, however, the relief shift did not arrive.

The mum-to-be was pretty miserable and was doing her best to push out the baby. She moved about the box stall in a restless way. She would lie down and then get up and walk around and around, as if trying to get away from the problem. By 2 a.m. I noticed that those two hooves had not come out any further. This concerned me, because they should have been making steady progress out. Most cer-

tainly the mum would need help. I began to feel irritated
and to wonder why Rodney, who knew about the imminent
birth, had not come to check on her and at least offer help.
So I left the barn and went to Rodney's quarters and
knocked on his door. No answer. I knocked again. Still no
answer. I opened the door, calling "Hi there!" Loud snores
greeted me. I opened the door, looked inside, and my gaze
met a sea of beer bottles. In the midst of them, sprawled out,
dead to the world, was Rodney. Drunk as they come. I might
as well have been trying to wake the dead. I rushed back to
the barn, my bones almost frozen with the cold. There was
no point in calling the vet—he wouldn't be able to get there
in time. Like it or not I was on my own, and things were
getting critical.

It was obvious to me that I would have to help pull the calf
out of the mother, so I looked in the barn medicine cabinet
for the two small silver chains kept specifically for that
purpose. I could find them nowhere; they had disappeared.
Getting angry wouldn't help—I would have to improvise.
Fortunately some of the bales of hay had been tied up with
strong plastic twine; putting two pieces together in three
sets, I plaited a long slender sort of rope with a sliding loop
at each end, which would slip around each small hoof. Then
I got a long, heavy rope and, armed with these goodies, went
into the box stall to join the unhappy animal. I talked
soothingly to her and gave out the loving scratches before
going around to the blunt end.

My heart sank. The poor little hooves were dry and
cold—a very bad sign. A calf during birth is covered with a
thick yellow-coloured goo, which is very slippery, to help the
birth process. The fact that the hooves were now dry showed
that there was a long delay. Oh dear, it was all I needed.
There is only so much birth trauma a calf can stand. I gently
slipped the small loops over the hooves and tightened
them, then attached a heavy rope to the fine one. This was
for me to hold on to and apply tension. Every time the mum-

to-be pushed, the added tension would help pull the calf out. An hour later those damned hooves still hadn't moved, and my back was killing me. I needed more tension, so I wrapped the big rope around a barn support post. I could then plant my feet against the side of the stall and have it act as a lever whilst pulling on the rope. This calf had to be born soon or it would not make it, and the mother might not either.

Heavens, it was a big calf for a first one. I began to increase the tension. Desperation was setting in. The mum-to-be was obviously getting very tired, and she wasn't alone in that. She had been at it for many hours now and was almost past pushing. What could I do? As a last resort I heaved myself to my feet, my back in agony, and got (you guessed it) a bucket of grain. I pushed it under her nose and once again renewed the tension on the big rope, pulling with all the strength I could muster. It is quite extraordinary that even in the agony of childbirth, cows still eat. And, sure enough, she put her head down and tucked in. It seemed to give her that extra bit of enthusiasm she needed, so that as I rushed back to the rope, I felt another contraction. "Heave!" I screamed and gave a mighty pull, which brought out the calf's head. This was no time to give up or let go. Suffering screaming agony myself, I managed to keep the tension, pulling, and yelling "Heave" as loudly as I could. A few more huge pulls, and the calf was out to the hips. There it appeared to be stuck. But at least it was alive.

I paused only long enough to clear the birth mucous from its mouth and then went back to heaving. I was desperate and frozen stiff. Then disaster struck me—my back got stuck in a U-turn. Damn, damn, damn my back. I couldn't stand up, so I crawled across the box stall in absolute agony and managed to turn the calf slightly side-ways as it stuck halfway out of the mother. Then, as fast as I could, I crawled back to the rope, braced my boots against the stall wall and screamed a raving "Heeeeeeeave!!!!!" The

A very wonderful moment ... a new life.

desperation in my voice must have had some effect, because out the calf came, like a cork from a bottle.

My hands were almost frozen solid around the rope, but I managed to pry my fingers off it and crawl over to the calf. It was covered in the thick yellow birth mucous. The calf and I both were in a slippery mess with the birth-bag and poop and all. Its lungs had to be cleared and its circulation stimulated. As I lay alongside it, I began rubbing with all my might, and not a little desperation, along its backbone to stimulate its breathing. It was a hell of an effort. I was rubbing literally for dear life. Then, cough ... a couple of coughs ... oh, thank you, God, it began breathing. Once I had seen that the calf was alive, I gave in to the pain I was suffering and lay back almost unable to move. The new mother was exhausted, and so the three of us lay there oblivious of the poop, the blood, the afterbirth—and the whole mess we were in. It just didn't matter. The mother had made it, she was alive and well, and we had a wonderful new baby. A girl! It took about half an hour for each of us to begin to move again. After I managed to straighten my back, I saw to it that the calf was happily suckling its mother before I left the barn. Then I dragged my weary body back up through the deep snow to the house. It was nearly 4:30 a.m. As I reached the kitchen door, I looked back at the messy trail I had left in the white snow. God, I was an unbelievable mess. I couldn't go into the house coated in everything but the kitchen sink! So, I stood out in the snow and stripped everything off—every single thing. I didn't even feel the icy wind; I couldn't be any colder than I already was. Then I walked inside, away from the disgusting mess of the things I had had on. I would burn them later, when I found the strength.

Once indoors I helped myself to a triple rum, turned on the hot water in the bath and threw in every sweet-smelling thing I had. I can't ever convey what it felt like climbing into that hot comforting bath that smelled so good, thawing out my weary frozen bones. Oh, the bliss, the mental and physical relief. I will never have a more healing bath than I had that early morning before falling into bed.

Habit is a strange thing. By 7:30 a.m. I was back in the barn. There was our man Rodney, doing the barn chores. He was singing his head off. "Good morning," he called cheerfully to me, "we had a great calf during the night." "You're telling me," I replied and went back to bed for the day.

On another occasion a farmer pal came around when we happened to have a difficult birth. After long hours in the barn and a successful birth, we went elatedly back to the house to celebrate. It's always good to have a drink with a pal in front of a huge, cheerfully burning fire. We both had quite a lot to drink, and the more one tucks into the stuff, chewing the cud, the more interesting the conversation seems to get. Thus we became totally engrossed, and I was surprised when I glanced at the clock and saw that it was well after midnight. "Your wife will kill you," I said as we headed to the door. It was a crisp, snowy night. My pal, being full of good cheer, reached out to grab me for a fun good-night kiss. Shrieking with laughter, I dodged out of the way, and the game began. A merry old chase started around and around the Rolls Royce, parked just outside. As I galloped around it, huffing and puffing with laughter, I yelled over my shoulder, "I'm too old for this," and he bellowed in reply, "Then slow down!" More crazy galloping ensued, until we both collapsed with exhausted laughter in a pile of snow and settled for a pal hug and more shrieks of helpless laughter.

All cavorting aside, there are some really terrible moments in farming, that is for sure. One is losing a calf. I suppose one reason I pampered my critters so much was that I think nature is so cruel. It seems to be that things should have been arranged a lot differently (instead of dog eat dog, as 't were), and so I perhaps was on a one-person crusade against Mother Nature.

On one particular occasion, I had lost a calf. Needless to say it was winter, adding the problem of rotten weather to any run-of-the-mill problems that might occur. The calf had got stuck halfway out of the cow, and this time I just hadn't the strength to get it out before it died. It was an awful experience. I had whisked the dead animal out of sight of the mother so that she not have unnecessary stress, but there was now the problem of a huge mother with oceans of milk and no calf to suckle her. Something had to be done.

When I had got her comfortable in a box stall full of straw, I dashed up to the house to call a farmer and ask if he had a newly born calf I could buy to suckle the calfless mother and use up her milk. The big dairy herds often have young calves they don't want, because they breed for milk, not for the calf. They usually send the unwanted calves to be killed for veal—ugh. I can't allow myself to think about that.

Anyway, the chap undertook to bring one as soon as possible, and he was aware of the urgency of the matter. I understood that one might arrive within the hour.

Back to the barn I rushed, where I found the farmhand, who had belatedly arrived at the scene. I explained to him about the dead calf, which didn't seem to upset him unduly, and I also explained what we would have to do. When things get desperate, desperate measures have to be taken. I was faced with a huge and splendid $7,500 full-blood cow having no calf and an enormous bag full of milk. We would have to try to get the cow to accept a newly born calf as her own. To accomplish this, there was an absolutely dreadful task to be performed. In order for the mother to accept a calf that wasn't her own, the skin of the dead calf would have to be cut off the animal and tied on to the back of the strange calf. The mother would sniff the new calf, sense the skin of her own calf and be fooled into thinking it was her own. By the time it had suckled her a day or two, the skin could be then taken away and the mother, having already accepted the calf, would continue to allow it to suckle.

I told the farm lad that this was what we had to do, and to my amazement he stated quite firmly that he could not do it. I couldn't believe it. "But it's got to be done," I protested. "If we don't put the skin of the dead calf on to the new one, she will reject it." A fat lot that mattered to him. It was beyond my comprehension that in this situation he would not even try to help me. How could he have the gall to refuse to do something which was absolutely vital for both the mother and the new calf? I pleaded in vain and then went back up to the house in disgust and fury and sorted out the biggest knives I could find, including a machete, about two feet long. My thoughts of the young men of this country were not the most complimentary at that time, I can tell you.

I was stuck with it. The deed had to be done—it was as simple as that, and it was no good yelling and screaming at the chap. He had refused point blank to help, and the

problem wasn't going to solve itself. Somehow or other I
had to get a calf for that cow and get her milk taken from
her, or we would have another problem—milk fever. That
would be a two-thousand-pound aggravation, and the less
thought about it, the better. The night was snowy, and the
winds were howling around the barn. Fury had given me a
great deal of strength, and I dragged the dead calf out to the
barnyard, leaving the big barn doors open for light. I got it
over to where I had left the pile of knives and began
sobbing. As I picked up the machete, I was actually screaming into the night. Oh God, how could I stick a knife into a
dear little creature that I had so short a time ago striven to
save from death?

Where would I start? In agony, I plunged the knife into
the tummy of the dead creature and proceeded to try and
take the skin off it. I will never forget that moment. Words
can never describe my horror, fury, disgust ... loathing of
the situation and of my task, coupled with my indignation
that I had to do it whilst a perfectly strong young man stood
by and watched. Then a neighbour, a German man who was
an experienced hunter, arrived. That stupid thing called
"hope" leapt out as I greeted him. But again, to my disgust,
he would not help me with my task. He thought I was stupid
to be doing it whilst the farm lad just looked on. By now I was
just boiling over with indignation and hatred of men, and
only this enabled me to complete the task. I had just about
finished when a truck arrived and a new calf was delivered.

Having bought the calf, and got it into the barn, I had the
driver help with making holes in the skin and slotting string
through them. The poor little new calf didn't quite know
what was happening to it, having a skin tied around it. It
looked comically gruesome. By this time I was exhausted
mentally and physically, and so I told the farmhand and the
driver who had brought the calf that they must stay with the
mother and see that she didn't kick the new calf. At least
they agreed to do that. Then I walked away covered with

blood, carrying my assortment of knives, up to the house to shower and try to rid myself of the horror of what had just taken place.

Then I was violently sick.

It was quite amazing to me what I could in fact do, faced with a desperate situation. I was in shock the rest of the evening, but by morning there were too many new problems facing me to indulge in the luxury of shock ... and so it was back to farming as usual. There was the matter of seeing that the newcomer was making progress.

LIFE

One winter's morning I foolishly decided to sleep in, thinking that surely I could leave the present man in charge for one day. At 7:30 there was a knock on the kitchen door, and the man, Henry, announced that he had a problem down at the barn. Lightning quick, I got my gear on and shot down to the barn, where I found a newly born calf at the point of death, its fur frozen to it. The only way to help it was to bring it back to womb temperature as quickly as possible. The mother, obviously having had a difficult time, had not had the strength to lick it clean. As a result, it was covered with the thick yellow birth fluid, which was now icy, causing it to look rather like a huge popsicle. I asked Henry to carry it up to the house.

Once there, we set the frozen calf down in front of the fireplace. Time was of the essence. I asked Henry to light the fire. He wasn't the brightest chap in the world and had a problem with this. I dashed upstairs for an armful of large bath towels, my feet not touching the stairs. When I returned, Henry was still where I'd left him, seemingly incapable of movement. This was going to be a lone task. Ignoring him, I wrapped the calf in one of the towels and started to rub it vigorously. My brain worked frantically—how could I get it warm. Ah, a heat lamp! I left the calf and

A moment of awful doubt.

rushed out into the garage and brought back the lamp and
a long plank. I balanced one end of the plank on the mantle
piece and rested the other end on a kitchen bar stool.
Around it I wound the heat-lamp cord, so that the lamp's
warm, red glow hung directly over the calf.

Then I smelled something burning. Oh hell! I'd switched
the lamp on whilst it was still lying on the chesterfield, and
it had burnt a hole in the thing. Still, I had more things to
worry about than a burn-hole. Henry, it seemed, was content to stand and watch the chair smoulder. Ah me ... these
things were sent to try us. I returned to the rubbing,
concentrating on its back to stimulate its nervous system.

Injections! A newborn calf had to have three kinds of
injections. "E-Sell," vitamins A, D and E, to protect it against
White Muscle Disease, and an antibiotic. I laid the calf down
and dashed over to the fridge, grabbing the bottles I
needed. I opened the kitchen drawer in which I kept the

needles and took three out. Back to the calf. I laid out the goodies on top of the bar stool, filled each hypodermic, and in no time flat the calf had had its injections. It must have thought it was a pin cushion, poor thing. What a welcome to the world.

I unwound the now-gooey towel it had been wrapped in whilst I had been rushing around attending to the medical needs, then lifted its head and re-wrapped it in a new dry, warm, clean one. Back to the rubbing again. Oh God, its dear little ears felt like icicles! Cold ears are a bad sign.

"Henry, is there no way you can find to light the fire?" I asked. Some mumbling from Henry, and he disappeared.

As I worked frantically away, rubbing as hard as I could, trying to induce life back into the pathetic little creature, I thought about what to do next. Oh yes ... milk! Again I gently put the calf down and dashed over to the stove and put the milk on to heat. Then I rushed back to the calf. More rubbing. Oh God, the milk had boiled over! Frantic dash back to stove. I added brandy and more milk to cool it, then tasted it—uummmm, good. Back to the calf. I tilted its head up and poured the warm, boozy milk down its throat a few drops at a time. (If you're going to die, ducky, I thought, you may as well go out on a cloud.) It coughed and spluttered ... what wonderful sounds ... and actually moved as it spluttered. It's going to live! Oh, thank you, God. I re-doubled my massaging of its ribs.

Once those lungs had filled with air, we were away to the races—a few more coughs and its breathing became regular. Aglow with hope, I continued rubbing its fur, which was beginning to dry out. Again I checked its ears and noted with a thrill of happiness that they were now losing that dreaded icy coldness. This baby, too, would be all right.

HENRYS

The world, it seems to me, is overstocked with Henrys! One
of the few exceptions to this rule was our farming "rep,"
Handsome Henry. Heavens, how we farming gals' (or at any
rate, this farming gal's) hearts beat faster when Handsome
Henry popped in for a rep visit. Tall, lean, quiet, with
sparkling blue eyes; the strong yet gentle type … oops,
enough of this drooling. Anyway, they must be hiding that
sort, because I haven't come across many. I am about to
introduce more of the "Ugh Henry" type.

One December, when my new farm was under construc-
tion, the builder's wife came to me with a sorry tale about
this person Henry. Henry was on the crew building my farm.
Apparently he had lost his previous job and home and was
about to be fired by this woman's husband. Would I please
help Henry by employing him as farm manager. How awful,
I thought, to find oneself in middle years without either job
or home and with a wife to care for. The quality of mercy was
not strained, in fact it was overflowing—immediately I was
hellbent upon doing a good deed. I was so hellbent, in fact,
that it did not occur to me to ask for references, or indeed
to question why the builder himself had given him the sack.
Eagerly I invited Henry to take the job of farm manager. Yes,
of course, they could move in right away! What could I do

to help … oh, it makes me ill to recall it! Also, it did not occur to me to check if he knew how to do the job; I just took it for granted that if he accepted the job he was competent. What a total twit I was—but a twit who was soon to have a rude awakening.

Henry's wife, a delightful person, helped me in the house. She had a wonderfully cheerful disposition and did a great job. I loathe housework and was on cloud nine at how things were going—in the house. The place just gleamed as in former pre-widow days, when life was full and wonderful. It was so good to have happy company and to laugh and chatter away. I was so happy about the state of things in the house that it didn't occur to me to check out the barn. So, having got them installed, I took off with a happy heart for three weeks in Bermuda over Christmas.

When I returned, I went straight to the barn, as was my habit. It was late in the evening, and I just had time for a quick "Hello" to the Girls. I sensed immediately that something was wrong. I couldn't put my finger on it. Maybe it was a feeling in the air. I noticed, too, that many of the barn implements were broken. Further, I sensed that the Girls were discontented, a very bad sign indeed. Gone was the contented chewing of cuds. Heavens, it didn't look to me as if they had been fed. I looked around—good grief, there wasn't any hay in the barn; what was going on? I had told Henry before I had left that if we needed hay, he was to call and order it, and that it was important to give the supplier a good ten days' notice to bring it, in case of bad weather. My God, my critters were ravenous! My head started to pound, and then I noticed that they had not been de-pooped, and I started to boil with anger. On any farm, or at least on mine, each animal's bed was cleaned every morning. I reckon if you have animals in captivity, you owe them the dignity of keeping them clean. If you can't do that, you shouldn't have animals. This was a situation I could not ignore. I went to the house, to find out what the problem was.

There was no Henry, and his sweet wife was in quite a state. Apparently Henry had disappeared, and by the looks of the barn he had been gone for some time. I was wild with fury and indignation. How dare anyone treat my animals this way? "How could the fellow just clear out and leave them to suffer?" I asked myself, my brain boiling. All it needed was one telephone call to get more hay brought. His wife was obviously very upset and had done her best to cope, but it was a simply unbelievable situation and the very last one I expected to be faced with upon my return. Anyway, I thanked her for what she had done and immediately called the hay supplier, Mr. MacNutt, who by great good fortune happened to be home. In a couple of hours I was handing out hay to some very grateful mouths. Thank the Lord that Mr. MacNutt was also a cattle man who fully appreciated the desperate situation I was in. He immediately loaded a small truck with enough hay to last me a few days and brought it over. Seeing my critters positively diving at the stuff made my blood boil; I think that if Henry had appeared at that moment in time, I would have cheerfully throttled him.

Henry's wife helped me as I did the barn chores, and I felt very sorry for her, and the desire to murder Henry was something I could almost taste. The next day he still hadn't reappeared, so I did the barn chores again, and so it continued for the next three days whilst we waited by the hour for the reappearance of Ugh Henry. Possibly under-standably—from Henry's point of view—he sneaked back. I state that because I certainly didn't see his truck arrive, and, oh boy, I was on the look-out for him, I can tell you. I learned of Henry's return from his wife. It seems that he was ill and had had to go to bed, and so I had to relent and carry on with the barn chores. I didn't at that point in time know of his booze problem, I just thought he was a rotter, but if he was genuinely ill, fair enough, he should stay in bed. However, I still could not understand or forgive the lack of care and feeding of the animals. It was a complete puzzle to me.

The third day following his return, he simply reappeared in the barn as if nothing had happened, and joined in the morning's chores. My jaw dropped as I observed him—I couldn't believe it. How could he not say something? Anything ... "Good morning" even. Surely an explanation or even an apology ... It was an unreal situation. I didn't know what to do or say and so I did nothing. I ignored it. About ten days later he disappeared again.

By this time I realized that it was a booze problem, and very soon I learned the different stages of booze: Stage One, the disappearing act; Stage Two, the lingering absence; Stage Three, the home-coming—usually in the dead of night; and Stage Four, the "must go to bed because I'm ill." The last stage, Five, was the "back to life with bitterness and a need for vengeance," during which various implements would be hurled, with curses, around the barn, and anything which happened to get in his way took a pounding. I will never forget entering the barn upon one occasion to catch sight of the wheel barrow in mid-flight.

It was a crazy situation. I felt dreadfully sorry for his wife and so put up with a series of these episodes before getting angry—very, very angry! Let's face it, we all have our problems, and it doesn't hurt to try to put up with someone else's. However, enough is enough. Just how was I to deal with it?

Our Henry had just returned from one of these sprees when we had a very heavy snowfall. Henry's wife was helping me the day after he returned. We were in the kitchen, and it was close to lunchtime. The snow had stopped falling, the sun had come out, the sky was a wonderful blue, and the temperature even rose. As we cleared the kitchen patio of snow, I commented to her that it reminded me of Switzerland and suggested that we lunch together on the patio. She cheerfully agreed. To keep things simple, we cooked two-inch-thick beef burgers and french fries and added a salad. Henry was outside doing the snow-ploughing as we happily got the things ready for our snow picnic.

The driveway down to the road was some five hundred yards long, thus ploughed by tractor. Looking down the drive, I could see Henry perched on the tractor, head down, seemingly intent upon his snow-ploughing. Something about the look of him gave me a pang of concern, but I shrugged it off, hoping it was only a mild headache. We got out some of the summer furniture to make it fun. I called out to Henry when lunch was ready. Henry didn't answer. I called a couple more times. Still no response. Odd. Maybe the wind was blowing my voice away. I suggested to his wife that she call him, which she did. Still no response. Oh dear, my vague forebodings were now materializing. I realized that something was amiss but, not wishing to embarrass her, suggested that as he was busy, we would eat our lunch, and she could take his back to their place on a tray. As we ate our lunch, we were both silent and uncomfortable as we watched Henry's snow-ploughing antics.

As we chewed away, sitting in the very pleasant sun, I noticed, to my astonishment, that after the driveway, our Henry proceeded to plough the field. How extraordinary! However, I thought, he must be doing it for some reason; maybe it was best not to interfere. The last thing I wanted was another problem. It was a vain wish because the next thing I knew, Henry had disappeared. Oh, oh ... here we go again: Stage One.

Back to the "Henry's gone" routine. I went back to doing the barn chores and the caring and feeding of the animals, with his wife helping. A few days later one of the RCMP men popped in. I was always delighted to see them because, remote as my farm was, it meant they were keeping an eye on my place. Over a coffee I mentioned my problem about Henry, and the chap kindly offered to have a word with him. Gratefully I accepted. As luck had it, Henry happened to return as we chatted, and so the officer went to have a talk with him.

At this point I began to believe in magic. Hey, presto—gone was the nasty old "returning" Henry, gone the black face, the threat of broken barn gear. Suddenly there appeared a meek, head down, repentant "wouldn't do it again" Henry. Had the Age of Miracles begun? This miracle lasted for a full two weeks ... until Ugh Henry disappeared again.

Several days after his disappearance I was driving home along the miles of dirt road to the farm when I saw a truck halfway up a tree, or so it seemed. I recognized the truck as Henry's. What could it be this time, I wondered. I stopped the car, got out and found him roaming around the woods holding his head. "Oh, Henry," I said wearily, pointing at his truck. "Do you have to bird-watch at this time of year?" Too fed up even to get annoyed, I got him into my car and took him to the doctor to have him checked out. I then got another shock. Apparently our Henry wasn't allowed to drink a drop—he had a tin plate in his head (I hoped he had been kicked in the head by a cow) and was on constant medication. Heavens above, whatever next? I realized that until I could figure out what to do, I was lumbered. There was his wife to think about. It angered me that she should lose yet another home because of rotten old Henry.

During another of his absences, still in winter, with high piles of snow everywhere, I had just finished the evening chores when Henry appeared, staggering drunk and incoherent. Disgusted, I curtly informed him that I didn't require his help that evening. Then I rushed up to the house to change. I had been given a fifty-dollar ticket to something or other and didn't want to miss the occasion. In a great hurry, I bathed and put on a black-chiffon creation, with delicate evening shoes, donned an ankle-length blue fox-fur coat, got into the car and shot off down the driveway. Foolishly I had forgotten that I was a farmer and should have worn boots until I hit the big city, but here was one more lesson about to be learned. In any case old habits die hard, and some of us have to be hit on the head a bit harder to learn our lessons in life.

About three-quarters of the way down the drive there was a slight hump, and from the house it wasn't possible to see what was beyond it. I had assumed that the driveway had been snow-ploughed all the way down to the road. I was about to learn otherwise. As I picked up speed after leaving the house, over the hump I shot, to land, in a four-foot-deep snowdrift, at the other side of which was Henry's truck, lying sideways across the road. No, this wasn't happening! Here I was done up like a dog's dinner and stuck almost nose to profile with Henry's car in a pile of snow. I was fighting mad … oh, why hadn't I followed my instincts and murdered Henry? I was mad, mad, mad! I got out of my car in my finery and delicate velvet shoes and fought my way through the snow back to the barn, where Henry was crashing around on the tractor. It had come in for its turn to be clobbered.

Dancing around in a fury of frozen feet, I bellowed to him to bring the tractor and move his truck. The wind was howling and blowing; it was an awful night. After getting the message through to Henry, I turned and tried to get back to my car. Henry's wife came along, bless her, most concerned to see if she could do anything to help; so we got into the car. I started the car and put the heater on, waiting for Henry to bring the tractor and get his truck and the snow out of the way. It was only a matter of fifty feet to the clear road at the bottom of the driveway. As I rubbed my feet, I noticed that Henry was now on the tractor. I was mildly surprised that he had actually managed to manoeuvre it out of the barn but even more surprised to see him driving it at top speed, not on the driveway, but on the other side of the fence, in the field. He was charging down that field like a chariot racer, the big heavy bucket of the tractor bouncing high in the air.

Now I knew, and indeed Henry should have remembered, that stretching across the field, just before the level where my car was stuck, there was a ravine about six feet wide and five feet deep. Going at the speed of sound, our gladiator was bound to come a cropper. But there was no

way I could get there in time to warn him, and the howling
gale blew my voice away. In slow motion, I watched the
inevitable: Henry landing in the ravine out in the field.
Somehow he managed to stay on the tractor as it went down
into it—and stayed there.

Blind fury took away the pain of the cold feet. I leapt out
of my car, climbed down the ditch at the side of the
driveway, which was full of mud and melted snow, then
climbed (with gritted teeth) the five-foot bank on the other
side, crawled under the electric fence and waded through
deep drifts of snow to reach the Errol Flynn of the farming
world. My main desire, I've got to admit, was to throttle him.
It's amazing what you can do if you are hopping, blazing,
damned mad—amazing, indeed, how I could get across
that ditch and all the way to that tractor in my finery and
delicate slippers. I ordered our Henry off the thing, and
dressed as I was, I climbed up into the driver's seat. In the
bitter cold and driving winds, I managed to manoeuvre the
tractor, by using the bucket, over the ravine and up the
other side. As I got off, I bellowed at Henry to get his truck
out of the way so I could get out with my car. Then I
struggled my way back to the car, fighting back tears of cold.
As I climbed back into the car, I really thought my feet
would fall off; they were just about frost-bitten. As I mas-
saged my icy tootsies, my teeth clattering, I watched Henry's
progress.

He was now standing in the field, at the front of the
tractor. He had left the bucket of the tractor (which contained a huge heavy chain with an enormous hook on its
end) still lifted high in the air. Through the car window I
could see him reach up into the bucket and start to pull out
the long heavy chain. With mute foreboding I watched, as
head bent down, he heaved the chain out. Link by link it fell.
I screamed out to him to stop, but he couldn't hear me over
the wind. There was no way to warn him, nor was there time.
I could only watch with anticipation for the last link in the

chain to be pulled down, knowing that it would be followed by the huge hook.

Again, as if in slow motion, it happened. Head still bent, Henry pulled the last chain out, and the huge hook appeared and fell. Doi——ng! Ring-a-ding-ding-dong! Our Henry got the enormously heavy metal hook right slap-bang on the bonse. Possibly right on the metal plate in his head. It might have been comical if I had not been so absolutely furious. Getting out of the car, I watched as this chap danced around the field in the snow, holding his head. I began dancing around on the snowy road in a war dance of my own, and Henry's wife was dancing around too, like a demented hen. It was dancing time for one and all down at the old corral.

Eventually Henry did get his truck out of the way, I did get into the town to my event, whatever it was, and spring did come. I couldn't turn them out during the winter, with no home for them to go to. I was very concerned about what would happen to his sweet wife. Need I say, along with Shakespeare, it was a long winter of discontent.

THE ARREST

The "Min of Ag" in Nova Scotia (ministry of Agriculture) is extraordinarily helpful to farmers. Each district has an agricultural representative who does all he or she can to help and advise the farming community. Mine was named Gordon, and he was a very nice man, tall and quiet and gentle. One day, when he came to weigh the calves, I noticed with amusement that he wore gloves. When he took them off, I saw that his hands were white and well manicured, not at all like us tough old farmerettes with our calluses and stubby fingernails.

The Min of Ag offered many grants to encourage us farmers to improve our land and our herds. One such grant was for irrigating and upgrading the land. If, for example, a farmer spent ten thousand dollars on the upgrading, this grant would pay up to three-quarters of that amount. What could be better? All the farmer needed to do was get a properly approved person to do the work, pay them, get a receipt and then submit it for approval of the grant. The Min of Ag helped all they could by way of advice and guidance—who could ask for more? I applied for and was promised the grant subject to the various conditions, which I undertook to meet. I had a hillside covered with alders and a low boggy piece of interval land. Both were wasteland. I needed the low-lying land ditched for drainage and the hillside stripped and graded into a smooth slope in order that a new pasture could be ploughed and seeded with either grain or hay to feed the animals. I did everything which was required; I followed all of the rules. I got a man who was approved to do the work. He understood the regulations and agreed to do the job. He arrived with an enormous machine. I explained roughly what was required, then a chap from the Min of Ag arrived to direct the proceedings, so I left them to it. The only stipulation I made to the machine man and the farm lad was that they should do nothing which would jeopardize the grant. With a cheerful grin, I told them that if they messed up my grant I would lop their heads off, as we each had a beer and a happy chat out in the field discussing the job. The work carried out had to be exactly as the Min of Ag chap dictated. As the work progressed, I would occasionally visit and take them a cold drink or a coffee, then chat and admire what was being done. It was so exciting to see things taking shape.

Secretly I was tremendously impressed with the way the machine man, named Byard, worked. My word, he was as good a worker as me, I thought to myself, and I am few and far between, I can tell you. He was on the job at 6 a.m. and didn't leave until dark. "The world could do with a few more of us," I laughingly told him as we chatted one day. He did excellent work, and I was delighted with the way things were beginning to look. Eventually I just couldn't resist telling him how I admired the hours he worked, and then he told me why: that cunning old Min of Ag had a time-clock in the vast machine, and he got paid the number of hours he worked. No wonder he worked all the hours there were. My admiration shifted from employee to employer. There must be something to be said after all, I thought to myself, for government.

The work was at last finished. I thanked and paid Byard, delighted with how he had transformed the places he had worked. We had two wonderful new fields. Instead of a boggy interval of low land, we had rich soil and a delightful new stream which bubbled and sparkled its way down to the lake. I am a garden-a-holic, and this passion extends to all of my land, so every inch of the farm, manure pile and all, had to be as attractive as possible. Maybe I did take it to the extreme by personally planting more than 3,500 daffodils down the driveway and three hundred or so Scots pines. The aching back I got doing the work was more than rewarded in the spring by the ever-increasing blaze of yellow flowers dancing in the breeze, reminding me of the poem by the chap whose name I can never remember which mentions "a host of golden daffodils."

The day after the landscaping was finished, the farm man came to tell me that there was a man from the ministry of the Environment to see me. Splendid, I thought, I have always been most interested in the environment. I asked the farm man why my visitor had come. Foolishly I assumed it would be to tell me what a wonderful job I was doing. It appeared, however, that, unbeknownst to me, there had been a steady stream of these Environment people pestering my chap, and this one had finally plucked up the courage to take me to task. I was fascinated to learn this and wondered what the chap could want to complain about; my place was immaculate. I was soon to learn.

One look at our Man from the Ministry, and I knew we were in for trouble. He was short and narrow of shoulder and wore an ill-fitting, unimpressive brown tweed suit. He sported a Hitler mustache, very shiny brown shoes and, to top it off, had a handshake like a wet cod. Oh, oh, oooh dear—in fact, ugh! All of this and the poor chap hadn't even opened his mouth.

To hide my misgivings, I called out a cheery "Good morning, isn't it a lovely day?" My greeting was lost on our M from the M. His face didn't lose its pinched look. I asked the reason for the honour of his visit. Apparently a jewel of society, a lowlife called an "informer," had complained that I was ruining the environment. I was simply astounded. Giving him the benefit of any doubt, I asked, "Is this a joke?" No, it was not a joke and could he look around. Pause. "Certainly," I said and proceeded to show him around the place. Inside I was boiling with rage. Just who would have the unmitigated gall to complain about my elegant, well-kept farm? What kind of person would behave in such a way? Why would they, if they had a problem, not come straight to me and confront me? Why would anyone go behind my back and cause such upset and mischief? I am of the personal opinion that informers should be boiled in fish oil … no, on second thought, that is too good for them. Boiled in manure. No, that also would be too good for them.

Still, this chap was only doing his job; so I swallowed my fury, put on a polite face and proudly showed him our wonderful new fields and stream, which was happily doing its thing, bubbling and splashing its way down to the lake. It was my pride and joy. To my surprise my splendid new stream did not impress him one bit. I've got to confess that this miffed me no end. How could anyone, particularly anyone interested in the environment, not be as utterly thrilled as I was with the new stream and dry fields, where formerly there had been a boggy wasteland. I was quite mystified. However, I was willing to help things along. Making my smile stay on my face, I offered to dam the stream up here and there, creating little waterfalls and ponds. I offered to stock them with fish. Perhaps it was wrong to expect a grateful smile or any other such pleasantry. His response to this kind offer was just short of an actual snort. If I did that, he said, I would violate yet another rule. No gratitude, just more ludicrous red tape. It took a great deal of biting my tongue to stop my suggesting that he go dump himself in the manure pile.

However, an ex-Brit does not give up easily. "Do let me show you our barn," I offered, finding it a little hard to keep that smile in place. This little squirt said he wasn't particularly interested in cows. At this point, I will hand out a piece of unasked-for advice: never let a farmer of pride and passion know that you haven't the slightest interest in his animals—especially not when that farmer is armed with a very large bull. He was led, none too willingly, to the barn. I simply walked ahead of him, and if he wanted to carry on the conversation, he had to tag along.

It happened to be the day we were separating the young calves from their mothers ... Septemberish. Not a happy day in the barn. Any child suddenly wrenched from its parent will kick up a fuss, and my pampered crew were certainly no exception to the rule. All hell was letting loose in the barn. The air was filled with indignant howls, sad wails and agonized cries. Even mighty MacCulloch's dignity was wounded—and that's an awful lot of wounded dignity, I can tell you. He very much resented being put in a pen of his own, away from his many wives and children, and so he added his protests to the uproar. What more fitting music could we play for our not-too-merry Man from the Ministry.

I got him into the barn and introduced him to MacCulloch, my formidable giant, my young bovine of impressive blood lines. MacCulloch was brushed daily and petted and was in fact a darling, an absolute pussycat. A massive muscular monster, but still a pussycat. His enormous neck and powerful shoulders exuded a frightening power; there wasn't a lot about him that betrayed his gentle, affectionate nature. He did not look at all like the pussycat he was. A beast of such staggering proportions might intimidate even the most lion-hearted—MacCulloch certainly did our man from the ministry of the Environment.

I felt it was my duty to mankind to show our M from the M a little about life down on the farm. I would give him something to bleat about. MacCulloch was fed up with life at the moment, lying down in his pen on his thick straw bed, so at first our M from the M did not see him. I opened his gate and beckoned our visitor into the large box stall with its massive metal bars. Up jumped MacCulloch the Mighty with a devastating surge of power, eager for his scratchings! "Oh, oh, oh, why was I so bad?" I chortled to myself. There really is a gleefully rotten part of me! Just try, if you can, to imagine the glow in my heart to see the neat, narrow-shouldered pipsqueak from the Ministry recoil in horror at the sight of the Gentle Giant coming to life in his lair. The Min Man's leap out of that box stall was truly Olympian, I promise you. It was a sight not to be missed. No, he didn't want to take MacCulloch the Mighty for walkies, as I had asked. "That nasty man doesn't want to take you walkies," I explained to MacCulloch, giving him a scratch. MacCulloch rolled his eyes at the chap, who did another splendid leap in an attempt to disappear into the woodwork. I followed him out of the stall, closed the gate and then climbed up a couple of rungs of MacCulloch's box stall to scratch him a bit more before rejoining the M from the M.

With a hearty slap on the back, I told him, "You're in luck, we're separating the youngsters today." Then, without waiting for his reply, I went on, "Just stand where you are and hold your arms out wide—don't let any of them go past!" With that, I turned and walked to the other end of the barn. I had carefully closed the big barn doors behind us and slipped the latch when we entered the barn, so there was no quick way out that our M from the M could see. At the other end of the barn I opened the gate of the enclosure in which the youngsters had been penned away from their mothers. They might as well have a spot of fun rushing around and dashing up and down the barn harmlessly for a bit. They certainly couldn't go anywhere. Our M from the M didn't know that, of course. All he could see was a mighty throng of beasts charging towards him at break-neck speed. Possibly a disturbing sight.

In fact, all he needed to do was say "Boo," and they would have turned and rushed back in the opposite direction. But alas, no one told him to say "Boo." I didn't oblige, that is for sure. Oh, Lord above, forgive me for the joy of heart I felt at the terror my young Ladies put into our M from the M! He turned and fought his way out of that barn. You've never seen a chap wrestle with barn doors as he did or run as fast as he did once out. I didn't even get to say goodbye to him. His car was gone by the time I had stopped laughing. Best of all, I had caught a last glimpse of those shiny brown shoes, and they were shitty, just wonderfully covered in poop. Perhaps there is justice in this world after all.

The next day the young man from the Min of Ag who had directed the land improvement arrived to apologize for having made a mistake about my grant. "What mistake is that?" I asked over a coffee at the kitchen bar. He was a pleasant young man, but I didn't really want to know about any mistake. I wanted the grant money. We had done everything they had directed us to do. Now it was their turn to live up to the bargain.

Two days later the young man's superiors came in a truck to inform me that they most certainly did not give grants for digging up streams. This was interesting, as we hadn't dug up any streams; rather, we had dug out the rubble which had been put in the original stream some fifty-three years previously when it had been re-routed causing the field to become bog, proving that you shouldn't mess with Mother Nature. I told them I was not about to argue the toss, and would they please cough up the grant they had promised? Then I left the scene of battle. I was getting bored with all of these dreary men and their hassling. And it was all because of the Informer, that dregs-of-the-earth rat. I have no time for people who attack other people behind their backs, because they do not have the honour and honesty to deal face to face. How anyone can take any notice of these despicable people, I do not know. I was venomous about the whole thing.

I think it was about two weeks later that a tall, charming chap knocked at the kitchen door. I was washing out the milk bucket, having just come up from the barn, where I had milked the Jersey cow. "Hello, who are you?" He introduced himself. Ye Gods! It was another Man from another Ministry!" This time it was the ministry of Fisheries. "Sorry, we don't grow fish," I said cheerily. "We've got a lot of bull around here, but fish we do not have. But as you are here, and it's coffee time, would you like a coffee?" Yes, he would, please. Well, it was a pleasant start; my kitchen bar is a most hospitable place, and at least this M from the M didn't have a small neat mustache and small neat, shiny brown shoes.

He didn't attempt to come over and sit at the bar. He stood where he was. I sensed that there was something wrong. A little shame-facedly he said, "I'm afraid I have to warn you that you have the right to remain silent ..." "WOT?" He continued, "You may wish to have your lawyer present ..." Holy gramoly, what was coming next? I finished filling the electric kettle in silence, then turned towards him, giving him my full attention. Very firmly I said, "Look here, I don't know what this is all about, but I certainly have no intention of bringing my lawyer all the way out here, and I can tell you that the last thing in the world I could ever do is remain silent, ducky! In fact, I am possibly the best chatter you'll ever meet. What is all of this about?"

The chap, in a state of great embarrassment, told me he felt like an idiot being there, but he had been instructed to visit officially. The crux of the thing seemed to be that he was a sheriff, and to prove it, he turned his coat lapel over. Sure enough, there was a badge marked "Sheriff." I took one look at the badge and started to giggle, eventually collapsing with laughter over the kitchen bar. What a riot, it was too much! I was being arrested. Never having been arrested before, I didn't know what to do. In any case, I couldn't stop laughing. In between shrieks of laughter, I held out my wrists, saying, "I give in, I give in!"

With a red face, he told me that he was not alone. Dear God, I looked out of the window and saw that he had a posse of two outside. This couldn't be real, it was surely something out of the movies. More helpless laughter from me.

How on earth could anyone take this kind of thing seriously? I continued to hoot with helpless laughter, and the poor chap continued to look highly embarrassed. Arresting someone who can't stop laughing is very difficult. I felt sorry for him. He explained that the three of them had found seven trout up my lovely new stream. This news highly delighted me and didn't seem to be any kind of a crime. "How ludicrous can things get," I wondered. "Don't worry, you could only be fined one hundred dollars," he said, hoping to give me some comfort.

"Wrong," I returned, "I would gladly go to jail for one cent on a matter of principle." What an outrage, getting clobbered for having dear little fishes happily swimming up my splendid new stream! He told me that one of the chaps outside was on the local council and was behind the whole thing and that he himself was only doing as he was told. He was obviously most upset at his appointed task. I quite understood. "Don't worry," I said, starting to giggle again. "You could even do me a favour. If I do have to go to jail, you might see to it that I go to the men's jail. I may as well have fun." That broke the atmosphere. "It isn't every day," I said, "that a tall, handsome chap pops in to arrest me." We both laughed, and he heaved a sigh of relief that his disgusting task was over with.

The arrest forgotten, we enjoyed a chat at the kitchen bar about farming and this and that, and then he left. It was a pleasant visit. After he left, I wrote an angry letter to the local councillor, pointing out to him that the very least he could do was approach me directly if he had any complaint. Needless to say, I received no answer from the despicable coward.

They did hold up the payment of my grant, but I dug my feet in. It took a year of legal battling, but at last my grant was paid. An ex-Brit does not go down under pressure, oh no! I would fight the world to the death on a principle if I felt I was right.

A couple of weeks later the same chap called around

again. "Oh hello, it's you," I said, holding out my hands once again for the handcuffs. "I give in again," I said. "No, please," the dear man said, "I was ordered to come." "What for?" I asked. "Forget it," he said, "the whole thing is ridiculous." I was puzzled but didn't wish to make an issue if there wasn't one. Apparently he had done as he was told: he had paid the visit and that, seemingly, was sufficient. I put on the coffee, and we had another most pleasant social visit. There are some people, thankfully, who don't have to arrest people to make themselves feel bigger and better. This chap, in any case, seemed to be in a more distinguished league than our original M from the M. At least he had a sense of humour. And he didn't have small neat, shiny brown shoes—God, how I detest small neat, shiny brown shoes.

I didn't get arrested, I did get my grant paid, I did have two splendid new fields, and above all, I had a wonderful sparkling stream where those dear little fishes could swim up and down to their heart's content. I often wonder if the M from the M got the poop off his shoes. I doubt if I will ever see him again; I sincerely hope I don't.

THE DINNER PARTY

It may seem that my farming life was one long hassle, and I suppose in one way it was, but that was only one-half of it. The other half was full of wonder, joy and fulfilment, along with a great deal of hard work. There is food for the soul in caring for (and being cared about by) animals, especially if one is quite alone. There is the incomparable thrill of a new birth and the delight of growing things. I can never quite get over a wizened little seed turning into, say, a beautiful flower; that always thrills me. No matter how elegant one's lifestyle is, those simple things remain.

Interestingly enough, the simple chore of leaning over a gate to inspect the herd warms the heart. The hard work of hay-making is a labour of love: labouring in the sun, stacking up bales on the wagon and the ride home are wonderful delights, as is the sweet smell of the newly stored hay in the barn. I am so grateful for everything about my farming life. I think I was very lucky to have had it.

However, becoming a farmer didn't mean giving up the elegant lifestyle I had formerly lived. Even whilst living alone, I dined formally, changing, after the evening's chores and rejuvenating bath, into civilized attire. Continuing what to me was my normal lifestyle after the day's labours kept me sane and stopped me from feeling like a cabbage.

A lot of people thought it extraordinary that I would wear an eleven-carat diamond when mucking out the barn or driving the tractor, but that was me. It may also be unusual to pet and groom one's critters dressed in silks or furs, but my cows were used to seeing me in such dress and truly never expressed surprise. I confess that I irritated myself when, for example, a calf licked a new suede skirt, permanently ruining it. But that is life. I don't let such little matters worry me unduly.

Becoming a farmer also did not mean giving up formal dinner parties. On one occasion I invited the Lieutenant Governor and his Lady, a delightful couple, and about thirty other guests to dinner.

Unfortunately the day of the party, there had been a series of problems, and I had forgotten about the dinner. We had had two cows calve. After the first one I had left the current farm chap in charge, telling him most specifically to see that the baby suckled its mother while I attended to the second calving. The day had started just after 5 a.m., there had been no time for lunch, and I had just got back to the house at about 6:30 p.m. when the guests started to arrive. Then I remembered the dinner party. Help!

The place was a wreck. The kitchen looked as if a tornado had hit it. Thank goodness the house was large enough to have a formal end—I quickly put the lock on the kitchen so no one could get in and see the mess. I could see the first arrivals through the kitchen window all dressed in black tie and long dresses. It's interesting how one's mind works as a farmer. As I noted my friends' arrival, it crossed my mind that not only were they elegant, but they were also clean. That made me smile to myself. In former days I would never have had a thought like that. Glancing into a nearby mirror, I then thought, "It's more than you can say about yourself, MacCulloch." Then I opened a window and called out "Hi" to the approaching pals. "Had a problem or two, do go in and help yourselves to a drink, but don't dare come to this end of the house; the place is a wreck." Laughingly they returned my greeting; they obviously didn't believe me. Ye Gods, if they saw the conditions in my kitchen, they would never eat a thing I cooked in it. Having closed the big kitchen door and locked myself in with the junk and clutter, I frantically started vacuuming the place whilst I tried to think what I would give them to eat. Steaks. It would have to be steaks.

Living in the middle of nowhere, you get used to not shopping and instead keeping at least a month's supply of vittles on hand. We were OK for steaks; in fact, we had lots of them from our own beasties, thick, juicy steaks. No-one would complain about chewing their way through one of those. I had found that it is possible to barbecue steaks straight from the freezer, and that, in fact, cooking that way ensures that the centres do not overcook. I pride myself on being a super short-order chefette.

At the speed of light I tidied up, got the steaks under way and shot upstairs to shower and dress. I congratulated myself that when I had designed my farmhouse, I had put in two staircases, the formal one in the main hall and a back one leading directly to the kitchen. At the formal end of the house the splendid staircase rises the full two stories in a room that is some twenty-five by twenty feet and houses our great eight-foot family chandelier. At the back end, however, I could dash up and down and not be seen in my shitty gear. Finally, transformation complete, I came down to join civilization wearing a long silk gown. You would not have recognized me from the person in the barn, I promise.

Sadly my elegant stay was short-lived. I was just enjoying a glass of champagne and welcoming my pals when there was an interruption. It was the farm man, come to tell me there was a problem in the barn. Damn. Just when I was in the mood for a party. In my long silk gown, I went back to my guests to explain that we had an emergency down in the barn. "Dins" would possibly be a bit delayed. Being super

sports, they said, "No problem. What is going on?" I explained that I didn't know but was going to pop down to the
barn to find out. I didn't stop to change my clothes but ran
straight out of the house and down to the barn, calling over
my shoulder for someone to please watch the steaks. The
steaks were taken off the barbecue, and everyone—an
assortment of financiers, doctors (one a vet) and academ-
ics—followed me.

The problem turned out to be with the cow that had
calved earlier that day; the one I had left in the care of the
new farm man with instructions to see that the calf suckled
the mother. It is very important that a calf suckle its mother
almost as soon as it can stand up and get the first milk, called
"colostrum," which has very special qualities. I had trusted
the chap, having clearly instructed him, and therefore was
furious when I learned that he had watched the calf go
without suckling all day. He hadn't even mentioned it to
me, and I was there helping the other mother with the
difficult birth. I was annoyed at myself. I should have
checked and not trusted him, but how could he be so
stupid? I couldn't believe that although he admitted knowing that the calf hadn't yet suckled, he had done nothing.

Alongside me in the barn was a pal (a guest that night)
who I consider to be second to none in the world of vets. The
poor cow was in a terrible state. I had never seen such a
huge, swollen, tender-looking udder. Her teats were bursting with milk. She was obviously in terrible pain. What a
stroke of luck that the vet was there. He immediately
recognized the problem and offered to help.

The other guests were wandering around the barn,
fascinated, as we discussed what was to be done. Most of
them had never been in a barn before. Of course they didn't
at first realize the seriousness of the problem. One told me
not to worry about the meal; they weren't too hungry
anyway. Some of the men suggested that we have the
cocktail hour in the barn, so a few went back up to the house

and brought back the necessities to set up a bar on the spot. Everyone was excited and pleased to be a part of the drama.

The vet took me aside and said quietly, "We must do something about this right now. I need your help." Then he explained to us all that the only way to help the mother was to render her immobile. Demented with pain as she was in her present condition, she would attack anyone within reach, yet she had to be milked. As it was many hours since the birth, the calf had to be given the milk very soon or it would certainly die.

The vet always carried his emergency kit in his car, and so he disappeared out of the barn to bring in a tranquillizer. From a safe distance he managed to get some of the injection into the cow. My, what a way with animals that man had. Then he vaulted into the box stall, where the suffering patient was roaming around, trying to get away from her own pain. He managed to get a halter on her (a rope around her head to hold her), which he handed to the farm man, telling him to hold on to it, then had me hand him a long, strong rope with a metal loop at one end. This he managed to get around the cow and position just in front of her udder—a very difficult thing to do without actually getting his head kicked in for his trouble. That cow would have attacked anything in its state of awful pain, but it was beginning to calm a bit after the injection. Expertly, he slotted the rope through the loop and pulled it screamingly tight just in front of her milk bag. Oh God, it was even painful to watch. As the rope tightened, amazingly enough, it paralysed the cow's back, which prevented it from kicking. Still he tightened until I felt sure he would cut the cow in half. Then the cow fell over, immobile and unharmed, on to its thick bed of straw.

The vet then handed this rope as well to the farm man, who was already holding the halter rope. Then he (who, it must be remembered, was still in his formal dinner dress) turned to me and said, "Jump in here quickly, I need your help!" "Certainly," I said. I picked up my long evening gown, wrapped it around my waist (all modesty gone), and vaulted into the box stall next to where the cow lay on her side, her udder huge and bursting with milk. "We've got to get the milk out as fast as we can," said the vet. "You take those two teats, I'll take these two."

When milking a cow, you usually take one teat in each hand, but these were so swollen, so huge, it took two hands to reach around even one. The vet instructed me to take some from each, alternately, so that the tension was taken from both as soon as possible. We worked like demons, oblivious of our audience. We didn't bother with buckets, we just squirted the milk out on to the straw bedding. The main thing was just to get that milk out of her and ease her agony. It was quite incredible the way it came out in a strong steady stream. I think one pull would have made a whole milkshake.

The guests stood in awed silence as the drama unfolded. The tension was tremendous. I think we were about three-quarters of the way along with our task when the most unexpected thing happened. The stupid chap holding the ropes (for some reason known only to him) let go of them. No longer restrained by being held at the head, nor having its back paralysed and kick-proof, the cow came to life as if an electric current had been switched on. Holy gramoly! There were cow legs thrashing around everywhere—you've never seen two human beings move so quickly. Both the vet and I took wing, leaping out of that box stall. She was a hellion, make no mistake, but at least we had eased her pain. I could have cheerfully murdered the farm chap. Heavens, such feelings were almost becoming a habit.

There were great cheers from the pals, who had enjoyed the show enormously. They of course didn't realize that the farm twit had almost cost us our lives.

As everyone got a drink and started to celebrate, we repeated the routine. This time we recruited a guest to hold the ropes, and this time we had a container and collected milk for the young calf. As the cocktail party continued down in the barn, we attended to the mother and calf. It was surprising to me how little people know about even the basic facts of cows; I had really learned an incredible tip that night about the rope looped around the cow to stop it from kicking. It was later to save my head from being kicked off my shoulders many times during my farming years. I am lucky to have a pal who is both a splendid veterinarian and a fun guy.

Meanwhile, our night's problems weren't over yet. The calf had still not had the first important mother's milk and was generally in such a pitiful state that the vet suggested we take it up to the house to try and get it back to "womb conditions." It was premature, and the barn had been much too cold for it. Well, no effort was spared. The meal was temporarily forgotten. Someone brought up straw, and we all pitched in and made a bed for it in the utility room just off the kitchen. No calf ever had such V.I.P. treatment. My gynaecologist was also a guest, and he was put in charge of taking its temperature. No-one else could find it. The vet thought that it didn't have much of a chance at life, and the only thing to do to help it was to give it intravenous feeding (it was dehydrated). One of the guests had brought her daughter, who was terribly upset about the sick calf, as indeed a sensitive ten-year-old would be. After we had done all we could for the calf, she sat by it, weeping over it, for the rest of the evening, bless her. Oh, the tears that were shed over that dear little creature. If anyone cries, I join in—I can't help it. I promised her I would keep it alive no matter what. Without that promise, she refused to go home. In any case, I was quite determined that the calf was not going to die.

We did eventually get dinner—everyone joined in in cooking it. It was great fun because there was so much to talk about. Everybody wanted to know so many things. The dinner party was a great success. It was a good job my farm kitchen is large. With its huge stone fireplace and bar, it didn't really feel like a kitchen. Formality went to the four winds as we all crowded in and ate where we felt like it. Everyone enjoyed doing it that way, they were so excited about the evening's events.

It took four weeks, but that calf lived. It lived in the utility room for two weeks. Then after those critical weeks, it was gradually weaned out into the walkway, then the garage and then back to the barn. It grew up to be an incredible and wonderful animal—proof that tender loving care can win the day.

As my guests left later that night, elated and happy now that all was well, and having been rewarded for their efforts with a hearty steak dinner, I heard one of them remark, "Patricia always gives such 'different' dinner parties!"

THE SALE

Eventually I just had too many cows. Some would have to go. But how does one sell the children? How was I to choose which adored critter to get rid of? Even the thought was criminal, but I had to come to terms with the fact that the barn was full; it wasn't physically possible to get any more critters in. I had to convince myself that I must have a sale.

I couldn't compete with the splendid sales of Peggy Rockefeller or the other wealthy farming people in the New York State area, or match the wonderful set-up of Harvey Trimble's place in Calgary. However, I would give it a whirl. As far as I knew, there had never been a "glamour sale" of cows in Nova Scotia. I invited all of the farmers in the province who bred Simmentals to put one of their herd in the sale, to advertise their own herd, add to the event and boost the sale. To my surprise and delight they all, without exception, agreed to send an animal. I was so excited. This was a man's world, and they had accepted me.

It is just unbelievable what there is to do when arranging a sale. I think my brain almost burst with the strain. Giving a sale is a once-in-a-lifetime deal, that is for sure. The aggravation involved in just getting the printed programme right is mind-boggling. Every detail of every animal is of the utmost importance: not only who their mums and dads were, but the dad's dad and the mum's mum, and the grandparents' mums and dads, etc., etc. I began to realize that it was no less than a crime punishable by death to make a mistake about such things. And at the very last minute I found out that the printer had botched it all up, and it had to be re-done in a panic. The printer obviously didn't know a thing about posh cows and didn't understand how important every detail was. Beyond the genealogies, there was the arranging of where each animal would go in the programme. It was essential that each consignor be happily placed, so as not to offend anyone. When it seemed that the last hurdle was over, there came an unexpected blow. Is Fate never satisfied, we wonder?

It so happened that the chap working on the farm had never looked too well dressed, and I particularly wanted him to look OK for the sale. We were, after all, advertising not only our animals but also our farming operation. In the most discreet manner possible, I enquired if he would be agreeable to wearing special gear for the sale. I explained that it was because we were to advertise our herd. (You can hardly tell a chap that he looks a mess, can you?) He was very pleasant and understanding, and agreed to wear things bought for him. So off I went to the town. I had such an enjoyable afternoon choosing "man gear." I came back with all sorts of items in matching co-ordinates: weather gear, sweaters, shirts, trousers ... everything I could think of that would be needed for the occasion. I wanted it to be wonderful. I spent quite an amount, but only the best was good enough for my Girls, even though their mum was selling them.

After barn chores, one Thursday evening, the farm man came to collect his outfit. "Look," I said, "if you don't like these things, or if they don't fit, they can all be taken back. There will be no problem." Off he went with the armful of garments. The next morning I asked him if the clothes were suitable. "Did they fit?" Yes, I was assured, they were all great and fit perfectly. Amazing! Thank goodness he had liked them and I hadn't offended him. A woman has to be so very careful when dealing with a man in areas like this. And it was only ten days to the sale.

Yes, our man liked his new clothes very much, so much, in fact, that the very next day, after he got his pay cheque, he disappeared, and I never saw him again. It was a case of "have clothes will travel." I found it hard to believe.

I was still in shock when a couple called at the door, wanting this chap's job. She was a huge woman, a good deal older than the young lad with her. I didn't look twice. Anyone with two sound legs and arms to match was sent from heaven. It did alarm me the way she ordered him around, but it was not for me to interfere. He was a nice, pleasant lad. Admittedly without a clue, but something was better than nothing—and I was running very short of "cope-ability." I left them to settle in, my mind on the forthcoming sale and all of the arrangements I was trying to make.

The whole preparation was, I would imagine, very similar to getting ready for a battle. I know now that I would make a perfectly splendid general. All I need is the offer of the job. The day had to be planned down to the last-minute detail. Each consignor would be responsible for the care of his own animal, but I needed to organize my own team of lads for the day. I don't think I had more than an hour's sleep a night the few weeks preceding the sale—who had time for sleep when living a nightmare? The Army kindly lent me two huge marquees, in which breakfast and lunch would be served outside the barn, in case of rain.

The morning of the sale dawned. It was a wonderfully fine day—oh, the relief! All of the lads who were to help for the day had to be there by 6 a.m. because each animal had to be given a final wash and primp. I had spent the two weeks prior to the sale helping to clip their coats—a painstaking ordeal. It took hours to do even one, and with such a huge number, it was a colossal job. Sweet Sadie's primping was minuscule compared with an army of beef bevies.

The wonderful look of the day belied it, because problems started at dawn. For some reason the new farm gal decided to be difficult—she had undertaken to make the breakfast for the workers and seemingly had had a fit of tantrums. I didn't trust myself to find out why. To stop my brain from bursting, I got into the car and drove around for ten minutes. This got rid of the throbbing of fury in my head. Then the guests began to arrive, and many pitched in to help, bless them. My doctor's wife and the wife of an oil magnate and another widow made the enormous piles of monster hamburgers we were handing out for lunch. After checking that things were progressing well in the barn and that all of the farmers who had consigned their cows to the sale were happy with their arrangements, I went to see that my house guests were OK and discovered that my lifelong girlfriend Mary, who had come from England to stay following the sudden death of her husband, was in tears.

I assumed that it must have been grief which had overtaken her and, heartbroken for her, went and put my arm around her, trying to comfort her. Through the sobs and tears I heard, "Darling, I am so terribly sorry." My heart bleeding for her, I said, "Look here, I quite understand. It's the best thing to do, to cry it out." "No, no," came the answer. "I'm crying [sob, sob] ... because I don't dust." "WOT?" "I just don't dust," she managed to say before starting to sob again. At this, I fell about with relief and laughter. Dust? Who cared a hoot about dust? I never saw the stuff on principle. Good grief, I had more to worry about in life than dust! Mary had a splendid and elegant home back in the motherland, England, with all sorts of help, as also had I in pre-widow days, and she wasn't accustomed to doing any menial tasks around the house. She was used to everything being immaculate. And now she had noticed that thing called "dust." The poor gal had a lot to learn. "Is that all that's wrong?" I asked, holding my sides, trying so hard not to laugh too much. Seemingly it was. Oh, the relief! "Now, look here, stop crying immediately," I commanded, opening a bottle of champagne … "It's 'elevenzez' time around here." I was so happy that it wasn't her own emotional problem that had caused the tears. I managed to convince her that there was absolutely no point in worrying about something like dust, especially when one's children were about to be sold.

In actual fact, I was tremendously relieved that she wasn't crying about her husband. Possibly having been thrown into the strange farming atmosphere and preparing for the huge sale had done its trick and helped take her mind away from her personal tragedy. I didn't mind one bit having tears over dust—a drop of fizzy can soon make one forget about such dreary stuff. Having had no help around the house for so long, I had come to terms with such things as dust. I had long ago decided that dust was not going to run my life. I would see it when I wanted to and only then. Armed with champagne, my dear friend Mary went back to helping with the buffet we were laying on after the sale. She is a super cook and was delighted to do her bit for the event. Her "bit" was a gynormous, fantabulous feast feeding about four hundred people.

The final preparations were under way before the public viewing, which was to be from noon to 4 p.m. The cows were gleaming, the air sweet, the barn a hive of activity, and I was happily surprised that I wasn't needed. I wasn't accustomed to such luxury. The plan for bringing in the cows, leading them up into the showring, which we had had built in the barn, then back out to their waiting pens had been tested and would work, and it was with great relief that I left things with the many experienced farmers there. Whew! Knowing that capable and experienced hands were taking over was so absolutely wonderful. It was arranged that during the viewing time there would be a free bar to get people into the party spirit, and we had a bluegrass band playing in the top of the barn, with a wandering minstrel twanging away on a

As far as I knew, there had never been a "glamour sale" of cows in Nova Scotia.

guitar down below. The cows just loved the minstrel, and with the mountains of sweet-smelling straw all around, there didn't appear to be one spot of poop anywhere in sight. I found that quite incredible; however, the great and terrible day was on its way.

The King of Beef, as I called him, Handsome Harvey Trimble and his charming wife had come all the way from Calgary to honour the event, the Minister of Agriculture had come to open the proceedings, and the official ladies all had bouquets. All of the pals helped officiate ... even the Lieutenant Governor and his Lady helped serve in the bar in the top of the barn, and we all danced and partied until the event began. Someone had given me a ten-gallon hat which I thought I looked quite splendid in. The pre-sale party was wonderfully successful.

Then came four o'clock. There were the speeches and then the giving of the flowers. After I had given my welcome speech and the sale was declared officially open by the Minister of Agriculture, the sale proceeded. I fled to my bath, to the comfort of the bubbles and sweet-smelling bath oils, where I soaked for the duration of the sale, armed with a magnum of champagne. I couldn't bear the misery of my Girls being sold ... I sobbed into the champagne until the sale was concluded. I just couldn't go anywhere near the barn, and the darlings I had just betrayed by selling them.

When the sale was over, many of those who attended came up to the house to celebrate. Apparently it was a great success, but it held no joy for me; I was just glad when it was over. I had to face those critters who remained. I dreaded seeing the looks on their faces—at that point in time I hated farming.

THE END

Well, the circle finally comes around. Eventually I ran out of money. All good farmers eventually run out of money. Like the joke about the chap who won a million dollars and, when asked what he was going to do with it, said, "I'm going to take up farming, and when I run out of money, I'll go back to work." My darling Girls had eaten me out of house and home.

The true farmers, we who love our critters more than we do life, keep them in the lap of love and luxury until the well runs dry. Our passion for the land and for our critters knows no bounds. Alas, my well ran dry, and at last I had to say goodbye to my Girls. I will forever feel the sadness of parting with them.

It is fascinating not being a farmer. When I wake up each morning (especially in the winter), for an instant I can't believe that I need not get up, don my heavy-weather gear and, braving the elements, get up on that tractor. Always I will loathe snow and ice. But always, too, I will die a little inside when I think of my Girls having to be sold. With them went a part of my soul. Yet what a luxury it is just not being a farmer …

Would I do it again? No, I think that eight years of farming have taught me that it really is not for a lone woman. It is just too, too hard a life. Yet I wouldn't have missed having my cows for anything. I just feel dreadful having had to get rid of them; I worry about whether they are happy and properly looked after. Quite often I pine, especially for Kate. Certainly no-one will look after them as I did, so I try hard not to think about them. What to do now? Who knows? Can one ever really get rid of that dreaded Cow Curse.

I think that when I die and go to Heaven (surely, in spite of all the terrible swearing in the barn, all of God's good farmers do go to Heaven), St. Peter will meet me at the golden gates, lay his hand gently upon my erring head and say, "Welcome, Patricia. Look what I have brought up here especially for you ..." There will be a herd of Simmental cows, and Sweet Kate will be one of them.

What of now?...

Put it this way: anyone looking for an ex-farmerette, a gal of great quality and incredible charm? My credentials are, "Have shovel, will travel."